Ultimate Flexibility

A Complete Guide to Stretching for Martial Arts

by
Sang H. Kim, Ph.D.

Turtle Press   **Hartford**

To contact the author or to order additional copies of this book:
    Turtle Press
    P.O. Box 290206
    Wethersfield, CT 06129-0206
    1-800-778-8785
    www.turtlepress.com

ISBN 1-880336-83-9
LCCN   2003026042

Special thanks to the photograph models:

Andrew Chasse
Ana Lourdes Gómez
Margaux Guidry
Brian Marcks
Karin M. Ravalese
Sheryl Ravalese
Carlos Sanchez

Printed in the United States of America

10 9 8 7 6 5 4 3 2

Library of Congress Cataloging-in-Publication Data

Kim, Sang H.
  Ultimate flexibility : a complete guide to stretching for martial arts
/ by Sang H. Kim.
    p. cm.
  ISBN 1-880336-83-9
  1. Martial arts--Training. 2. Stretching exercises. I. Title.
GV1102.7.T7K563 2004
796.8--dc22
                          2003026042

Preface

Be friendly with your body. Your mood and condition change hourly, daily, monthly and with the seasons. You've got to build up from wherever you are. You should not and don't have to compare yourself to someone else who is way ahead of you. Be yourself. Build from your honest self. You cannot cheat with flexibility. You either have it or don't.

The exercises in this book are those that I have practiced for over 30 years. Even now I have some degree of difficulty with some movements. So when you are struggling with a particular exercise remember that even after thirty years, I struggle too. Begin from wherever you can and work toward the ideals that you see in the photos. While some of the exercises are quite difficult, some are very easy. These are the exercises that you can and should do every day because they don't cause pain or require much effort.

Keep your stretching regimen interesting and relevant to your overall training. When you feel that your flexibility training is related to your martial arts practice, you will definitely progress toward your goal. Begin with what you can do well, then gradually challenge yourself before finishing with something pleasant and relaxing. Always end your workouts on a positive note so your muscles will be eager to try again and your mind will be fresh and alive.

The road to flexibility travels through both the scenic woods and the barren desert. Whatever you meet and wherever you find yourself, remember you are on a journey.

Happy Stretching!

Sang H. Kim

Contents

Chapter
One

Before we get into specifics about stretching and flexibility, let's take a moment to orient ourselves. If you are interested in improving your flexibility, you probably fall into one of three groups: the novice who is starting from scratch, the experienced martial artist who is frustrated with his or her progress or the elite athlete who is looking for every edge when it comes to flexibility.

Depending on your level of experience and knowledge, the way you approach your training and the way you use this book will differ greatly.

the Big Picture

...Starting from Scratch

You're new to martial arts and/or new to stretching and flexibility. You know you want to be more flexible, but have no idea where to start. Start with the list below:

1. Start slowly

Sure, you're anxious to get started, but flexibility is a long-term process. Doing twice as much today doesn't mean you will progress twice as fast or even that you can do half as much tomorrow.

2. Make a small commitment

Flexibility doesn't require a huge commitment. It's much less time consuming than cardio or even your regular martial arts training. By making a small commitment, you're more likely to stick to it in the long run.

Flexibility doesn't require a huge commitment.

3. Choose one exercise for each target area

You have roughly fifteen target areas that need to be stretched for martial arts training. Doing one exercise per target area is fine to start out. See the Core Workout in the Workout Section (page 268-269) for a good basic workout.

4. Spend no more than 15 minutes daily

Everyone, no matter how busy, can afford fifteen minutes out of the day for stretching. By keeping your time commitment small, it becomes hard to make excuses for skipping a stretching session. Fifteen minutes is plenty of time for a beginner to cover the major muscle groups. If you are alternating target areas, for example, the upper body one day and the lower body the next, you can either spend more time on each stretch or simply cut your session to eight to ten minutes.

5. Reward yourself

Stretching shouldn't be drudgery. If you don't enjoy it as a relaxing activity in itself, reward yourself at the end of each session.

6. Get educated

Read up on how stretching works, which exercises are beneficial and which are harmful, how to apply flexibility to your martial arts training and how to turn up the intensity as you progress. The Stretching and Flexibility chapters of this book are an excellent place to begin.

7. Make one or two short-term goals

Short-term goals are easy to achieve and will make you feel like you're progressing right from the start. Right now take a moment to set a goal of exactly how often and how much you'll stretch. Write it down using concrete words and imagery. For example, "Starting today, I will stretch for fifteen minutes every day right before breakfast." If you need help setting goals as you progress, the Planning chapter (page 80) has a number of helpful strategies.

Right now take a moment to set a goal of exactly how often and how much you'll stretch.

8. Evaluate your progress frequently

Sometimes, flexibility training can be frustrating because the results are hard to measure. Choose a few exercises to track your progress. Static stretches like the standing toe touch, hamstring stretch and side bend work well for beginners. As you progress, gauging your progress within the context of your martial arts training will become more important to you, but for now, just focus on a few simple tracking exercises.

9. Don't get discouraged if you plateau

Reaching a plateau, a point at which you get stuck for a short time, is normal. Don't let a plateau discourage you. Instead, see it as your body's way of saying, "Hey, challenge me – I'm ready!"

10. Stay within your depth

If you are participating in a martial arts class, it may be tempting to imitate the movements you see higher-ranking students doing or to jump ahead and start doing PNF stretches right away. Unfortunately, this is more likely to cause setbacks than improvements in your flexibility. While static stretching can seem boring and low tech, it is the safest and most effective means of stretching for a beginner. In time, as long as you stay injury free and progress steadily, you'll be the one that the new students are eager to imitate.

...Getting Over the Hump

You've been involved in the martial arts for a while, maybe even years, but you feel stuck. No matter what you do, your flexibility doesn't improve in the ways that you'd like. If you're ready to get on the road to measurable progress, here is your road map:

1. Educate yourself

Just because you've been stretching a certain way since you were a white belt, doesn't mean you're doing it right. There are many theories on stretching and simply understanding how your muscles work can be a big help in sorting out what theories you choose to apply to your training.

2. Set concrete goals

If you've always wanted to be "more flexible," but have never really been sure what that means, now is the time to get serious. Set a minimum of three concrete flexibility goals for the coming year. For more details on setting and sticking to your goals, see the section on goal setting (pages 86-92).

3. Make a plan

Once you have goals, you need a plan. Simply deciding that you're going to stretch after each class isn't enough to help you overcome your frustration. By the time you finish this book, you should be able to create a plan that tells you exactly how you're going to take your flexibility to the next level, including which exercises, how often, using which methods of stretching, when and at what intensity level. The more specific you can be in planning, the better your chances of increasing your flexibility. If you have never planned a workout before, the Planning chapter has detailed instructions to help you get started.

The more specific you can be in planning, the better your chances of increasing your flexibility.

4. Cut out what's not working

Some stretches just plain don't work. You may be doing them out of habit or because you've always done them, but now it's time to cut them out of your training plan and replace them with what works for you. Remember, what works for the guy next to you in class or what works for your instructor, may not work for you. Listen to your body and experiment.

5. Keep a training log or diary

When you feel stuck, a training log or training diary can help you pinpoint the source of your frustration. In writing down what you do and how you feel after a workout, trends may emerge. Finding a training style that works for you takes some detective work, but it's well worth the effort. More details about creating a training log that really works can be found on pages 89 and 90.

6. Change your routine

Routines are comfortable, but they often lead to stagnation and boredom. In this book, you'll find a wide variety of exercises for each area of the body. Don't wait until you're tired of an exercise or training routine to change it. Give your training plan a facelift at least once every three months to keep it fresh and exciting.

7. Be honest

Are you really doing what you planned? It's easy to cheat a little here and there and then find yourself scratching your head at the end of the month when you don't see the progress you expected. Did you really spend ten minutes on stretching today or was it more like seven? Did you hold each stretch for twenty seconds or get bored and trim it to ten? By being honest with yourself, you can accurately evaluate the effects of each exercise.

8. Guard against overtraining

When you are eager to improve, you risk pushing yourself too hard. When it comes to flexibility training, doing twice as much today doesn't mean you can skip tomorrow. And doing twice as much two days in a row, might mean your muscles end up tighter instead of looser. Develop a reasonable workout plan and stick to it.

The bottom line is, if you want to be more flexible, stretch every day. There are no shortcuts.

9. Avoid gimmicks

Sometimes when you get stuck, you'll try anything to get out of a rut. There are plenty of "quick results" gimmicks out there. Use this supplement or try this machine, they say, and cut days off your training. If it sounds too good to be true, it probably is. The bottom line is, if you want to be more flexible, stretch every day. There are no shortcuts.

10. Stick with it

When you are past the beginner stage, but haven't broken through to your ultimate level of flexibility, progress may seem slow at times, but don't give up. You will get there!

...Achieving Ultimate Flexibility

You're at the top of your game and need every edge. Start here:

1. First, congratulate yourself

As an experienced martial artist, you are not only in great shape, but you're in touch with your body. Knowing what your body is telling you makes it much easier to push yourself to your ultimate heights.

2. Understand and use advanced techniques

If you are at a better than average fitness level, you are ready to use advanced stretching techniques like PNF stretching and dynamic stretching. These techniques carry a greater risk of injury for the average athlete, but for conditioned athletes, they result in better quality results in less time. More information about advanced techniques can be found in the Stretching chapter (page 27).

3. Do the research

Use this book as a jumping off point to discover areas that interest you. There are many areas of training and physiology that are beyond the scope of a general stretching book. When you read something that interests you, make an effort to find advanced research and delve more deeply into it.

4. Get a coach or trainer

Advanced techniques like PNF stretching require hands on training. There is only so much that you can learn from a book or video. If an advanced technique interests you, spend a few sessions with a coach or trainer to discover how it works and how to apply it correctly and safely to your training.

5. Specialize

Go deep. As an advanced martial artist, you have the experience and know-how to specialize in an area that interests you and push yourself beyond the limits of your less experienced classmates.

6. Do only what works

Eliminate the fluff from your workouts. Once you reach the higher levels of martial arts training, the amount of knowledge you need to maintain through practice can feel overwhelming. There's no need to do dozens of stretches if you have ten that work your whole body adequately. That's not to say cut corners, but just because you've done fifty side kicks as part of your warm-up since you were a white belt doesn't mean those kicks are still contributing to your workout. As your skill level increases, your training methods need to keep pace.

As your skill level increases, your training methods need to keep pace.

7. Multitask

Can you accomplish more than one goal through the same training method? For example, can you stretch and strengthen certain muscles at the same time? Can you work your stances and stretch your hamstrings? By finding ways to make the conditioning portion of your training multipurpose, you'll free up more time for skill related training.

8. Understand how training impacts your flexibility

Strength training will make you more flexible.

Did you know that strength training will make you more flexible? How about the effects that flexibility has on plyometric training? By educating yourself about the impact of various aspects of your training, you can train smarter and avoid "robbing Peter to give to Paul."

9. Have fun

Flexibility isn't just about measuring your splits or pushing for another three degrees of range in your axe kick. When you are highly flexible, a whole new area of the martial arts opens up for you. This is the time in your training to push yourself to new heights. Have you ever wanted to learn acrobatic moves? Flips? Multiple kicks? Properly trained muscles are half the battle when it comes to moves with a high degree of difficulty. When we talk about applied flexibility, this is where the rewards lie. Treat yourself to some fun in your training as a reward for your hard work.

10. Share your knowledge

If you have a solid understanding of flexibility training, why not share it? Whether you are an instructor or a skilled student, you are in the position to help the students at your school achieve ultimate flexibility too.

Chapter
Two

Flexibility is the ability to move your muscles and joints through their full range of motion. When it comes to martial arts, the range of motion required for advanced movements often calls for greater than average flexibility. One of the first things you learn as a martial artist is how to stretch your muscles to increase your flexibility. While some people find that their flexibility progresses on track with their advancement in the arts, others find flexibility an ongoing source of frustration.

Flexibility

◎ What is Flexibility?

Flexibility is the ability to move your muscles and joints through their full range of motion. When it comes to martial arts, the range of motion required for advanced movements often calls for greater than average flexibility. One of the first things you learn as a martial artist is how to stretch your muscles to increase your flexibility. While some people find that their flexibility progresses on track with their advancement in the arts, others find flexibility an ongoing source of frustration.

How flexible you are depends on a number of factors. Some you can change: frequency and intensity of stretching, choosing the right exercises and executing them correctly, increasing strength with flexibility, overall conditioning. Some you cannot change: genetics, body structure, a serious injury or disability, age, gender. The good news is that the average person can make substantial gains in flexibility through a regular stretching program.

Research has shown that flexibility is not a general characteristic that someone possesses but is specific to each area of the body. For example, you might have great upper body flexibility but be tight in the legs or vice versa. In fact, many martial artists even find that their right hip is more flexible than the left allowing them to naturally kick higher on one side than the other. Ironically, once you begin to favor one leg over the other, the more flexible leg will continue to become yet more flexible and the other side may start to lag farther behind.

The only way to increase your flexibility is through targeted physical activity that lengthens the muscles.

Perhaps one of the reasons that flexibility is not an inherent physical trait relates to the way it is gained and lost. The only way to increase your flexibility is through targeted physical activity that lengthens the muscles. Conversely, inactivity of those same muscles causes a steady loss in flexibility. Stretching is not something you can do for six months and then forget about. It needs to be done at every workout for as long as you pursue your martial arts training and, ideally, for the rest of your life, in some form or another.

Factors you can change	Factors you cannot change
Frequency of stretching	Genetics
Intensity of stretching	Body structure
Choosing the right exercises	Age
Correctly excuting excerises	Injury or disability
Building strength	Gender
Overall conditioning	

Why Greater Flexibility Can Make You Stronger and Faster

Thanks to something called the stretch-shortening cycle, your body had the ability to briefly store and utilize the tension created by a rapid muscle stretch. A very simple description of the stretch-shortening cycle likens it to an elastic band. When you stretch the elastic, it becomes taut and ready to snap back with force when released. The more pliable the elastic and the farther you can stretch it, the more force it will generate when released.

In your muscles, the process is slightly more complex, though based on the same principle. When a muscle lengthens rapidly, it stores a reserve of potential kinetic energy, which can then be delivered much more effectively and with less expenditure of effort than a simple concentric contraction.

Imagine the motion of a baseball pitch. The pitcher lengthens his arm to an almost superhuman position, then at the maximum point of stretch contracts his muscles to propel the ball. Now imagine how much less powerful his pitch would be if he simply lifted his arm slowly behind him, stretched and then threw the ball with a simple concentric contraction of his arm muscles. The dynamic nature of the pitch would be lost. By achieving a full stretch and triggering the stretch reflex of the opposing muscles to begin the propulsion of the ball, his flexibility increases his power and speed of movement substantially.

Many athletes, including martial artists, use plyometric exercises as part of their training to take advantage of the stretch-shortening cycle. Even if you choose not to use plyometrics, your increased flexibility will contribute to the speed and power of your martial arts movements.

◎ Influences on Flexibility

There are a number of factors that influence an individual's flexibility:

1. Age

Flexibility declines as you age, but much of this decline is related to a decrease in physical activity. With regular stretching and exercise, much of the age-related decline in flexibility can be prevented or even reversed. If you are older and have been inactive, it may initially take more time to see gains in your flexibility training, but stick with it. In time, you can attain the same level of flexibility as your classmates in their twenties and thirties.

2. Gender

In general, women are more flexible than men, particularly in the spine, hips and thighs. In addition to a different bone structure in the hips and spinal area, women have higher levels of estrogen and progesterone, which help maintain flexibility, while men have higher levels of testosterone, which is geared toward building and strengthening muscles. On the other hand, men tend to have stronger upper bodies, particularly in the arms, shoulders and abdomen. This makes certain supported and dynamic stretches easier to perform. As a side note, stretching can reduce pain and discomfort that women experience during menstruation.

3. Location

Flexibility is site specific, meaning that it must be developed in each area of the body individually. For example, a professional baseball pitcher can have an extremely flexible pitching arm, while his other arm might have the flexibility of the average athlete. Some joints have greater potential for flexibility. The shoulder, for example, is flexible to the point of endangering itself while the hip is sturdy and much less susceptible to being overstretched.

4. Activity Level

A more active person will naturally be more flexible than a sedentary person and a person who has a lifelong habit of athletic participation will be more flexible than someone taking up a sport late in life. One of the key factors in developing and maintaining flexibility is consistent activity.

5. Temperature

When the body temperature is raised through activity, such as a pre-exercise warm-up, the body becomes more elastic. As the body cools, elasticity decreases. If you take a break in the middle of your workout and your body cools down to pre-exercise levels, spend a few minutes jogging in place or doing some other light aerobic exercise to re-elevate your body temperature before continuing with your workout.

6. Strength Training

The correct strength training exercises increase, rather than decrease, flexibility. Choose weight or resistance training exercises that work muscles through a full range of motion.

7. Pregnancy

During pregnancy, the body releases a hormone called relaxin to loosen the joints and ligaments in preparation for childbirth. During this time, women should be especially careful when performing stretching or other exercises that place undue stress on the joints.

8. Intensity and Frequency of Stretching

Quite simply, how much you put into your stretching will equal how much you get out of it.

9. Exercise Selection

Choosing a dozen exercises that target the muscles you'll be using in your training is far more effective than doing thirty poorly targeted exercises. Remember, you want to build flexibility that directly relate to your martial arts skills.

10. Technical Execution

Each stretching exercise must be executed correctly to have the desired effect. If you are cheating on a hamstring stretch so that you can touch your toes, you might feel better in the short term, but your hamstring flexibility will not increase substantially, no matter how often you stretch. Focus on doing each exercise correctly, even if it means starting with the beginner variations or achieving only a minimal stretch at first.

11. Overall Conditioning

Good overall conditioning will contribute to good flexibility and good flexibility is a major factor in maintaining an optimal martial arts conditioning level.

◎ Types of Flexibility

All flexibility is not created equal. For example, being able to do a split or a back bend does not mean you will be able to execute a straight up side kick. Conversely, being able to kick above your head doesn't guarantee that you can do a full split. Kicking requires functional or sport specific flexibility while a split requires static flexibility. Let's look at the different types of flexibility to see how they affect your martial arts performance:

Static Flexibility

Static flexibility is flexibility that does not involve movement. It is a measure of the range of motion about a joint. For example, to measure the static flexibility in your hamstrings and lower back, you can perform the sit and reach test. Sit with your legs outstretched and reach for your toes. By measuring at regular intervals how close to or how far past your toes your hands reach, you can track the improvement in the static flexibility of your hamstrings and lower back.

Other popular gauges of static flexibility are the standing toe touch, the back bend and the split. While these are interesting benchmarks, they do not measure what most martial artists truly want to achieve: functional flexibility. Research has shown that there is no direct relationship between static flexibility and functional flexibility. Functional flexibility tends to be much greater than static flexibility in movements that relate directly to those performed in an athlete's chosen sport. For example, a baseball pitcher who has an extreme range of motion when pitching probably cannot achieve the same range of motion in a static stretch. We will see why this is true when we look at the role that reciprocal inhibition plays in the relaxation of the muscles during any given movement.

Stability of a joint should always be a priority over range of motion.

It's also important to remember that martial arts is not a stretching contest. While flexibility is a fundamental necessity, too much emphasis on extreme levels of static flexibility can be damaging to your body. In any activity that requires quick changes of direction or rapid stops and starts, overly flexible joints can lead to strained or torn ligaments, tendons and muscles. This is why it is important to always build strength with flexibility and to engage in stretching exercises that strengthen as well as loosen the muscles. A correctly designed condition program uses strengthening exercises that enhance flexibility by developing control of the muscles at even the outer limits of the range of motion. Stability of a joint should always be a priority over range of motion.

Functional Flexibility

As already discussed, functional flexibility is the ability of a joint to move through a range of motion during the performance of a movement at normal or rapid speed. For example, throwing a spinning back fist requires good functional flexibility in your upper back, shoulder and arm. Kicking your opponent in the head with a roundhouse kick requires functional leg, hip and lower back flexibility.

Functional flexibility is directly related to individual movements. The fact that you can throw a high roundhouse kick does not guarantee that you can throw a high side kick. Each kick engages the muscles in your legs to varying degrees and requires functional flexibility in your hip at a slightly different angle. You may find that you and a classmate have similar levels of general flexibility but that he excels at high spinning kicks while your side kick is higher than his. Functional flexibility can be improved both through performance of the target movements and through targeted dynamic stretching.

Active Flexibility

This is a somewhat confusing term because active flexibility can be either static or dynamic and its applications to martial arts movements aren't easy to correlate. Active flexibility is the range of motion achieved without outside assistance. For example, a measure of active flexibility might be how high you can raise your leg in side kick position without assistance from a partner or stretching bar. Active flexibility must be demonstrated using only the athlete's muscles. Obviously, you are able to throw a side kick much higher than you can simply raise your leg into a side kicking position. With the assistance of a partner, you can probably achieve a height somewhere between the two. As a measure of flexibility for martial artists, active flexibility has little direct value.

So to summarize, for martial arts training, your primary measure of flexibility should be functional flexibility— how well you can perform your target movements. Static flexibility can be a useful secondary measure for goal setting, but should not be relied upon as an accurate gauge of performance.

Your primary measure of flexibility should be functional flexibility.

Chapter Two Q & A

What is Flexibility?

Flexibility is the ability to move your muscles and joints through their full range of motion.

My left leg is flexible but my right leg is really tight. Why?

Research has shown that flexibility is not a general characteristic that someone possesses but is specific to each area of the body.

I'm really flexible. Do I still have to stretch?

Yes. Flexibility is not an inherent physical trait. The only way to increase or maintain your flexibility is through targeted physical activity that lengthens the muscles. Inactivity of those same muscles causes a steady loss in flexibility.

Will strength training make me less flexible?

No, just the opposite, thanks to the stretch-shortening cycle. A very simple description of the stretch-shortening cycle likens it to an elastic band. When you stretch the elastic, it becomes taut and ready to snap back with force when released. The more pliable the elastic and the farther you can stretch it, the more force it will generate when released.

What influences how flexible I am?

A number of factors including: age, gender, area of the body, general activity level, atmospheric temperature, overall condition, stretching and how much strength training you engage in.

Why can I do a full split and still not be able kick above my head?

Static flexibility (as in a split) does not involve movement and therefore does not necessarily translate to functional flexibility, which is the ability to move a joint through a range of motion during the performance of a movement at normal or rapid speed. For martial arts performance, functional flexibility is the most useful measuring tool.

Chapter
Three

While stretching and flexibility are often used interchangeably by novice athletes, they are two very different concepts. Stretching is a means to improve your flexibility, but it is not necessarily the only means. If acheiving flexibility for martial arts is like building a house, then the various forms of exercises are your building blocks.

Stretching

◎ Benefits of Stretching

In addition to increasing the flexibility of your joints and muscles, stretching has a number of beneficial "side effects" that will improve not only your martial arts performance, but other areas of your life as well.

Overall Fitness

Flexibility is one of the keys to a long and healthy enjoyment of the martial arts. Through regular progressive stretching, you can increase the height of your kicks, the power of your throws and the effectiveness of your ground fighting. Properly developed total body flexibility is essential to improving the speed and power of your techniques as well as preventing common injuries, like sprains and strains. When you stretch at every workout, you will progress faster and recover from workouts more quickly.

Increased flexibility not only leads to improved performance, it makes you feel better in general. When your muscles are limber, your posture improves, you have less difficulty performing everyday tasks, you breathe more deeply and naturally, and you feel less stressed throughout the day.

Improved Body Awareness

Through consistent, mindful stretching you develop and strengthen the connection between your mind and your muscles. Each stretch creates a distinct sensation in a specific set of muscles that you use in your martial arts practice. By paying careful attention to these sensations, you will develop a detailed knowledge of how your body works, which muscles are used for what type of movements, how your muscles and joints interact and where your weak points lie.

When you stretch at every workout, you will progress faster and recover from workouts more quickly.

Increased Energy

Chronically tense muscles have reduced circulation, resulting in a lack of needed oxygen and a build up of waste products in the muscle. This combination can leave you feeling sore and fatigued all over. Stretching regularly improves circulation, bringing much needed nutrition to the muscles and taking away harmful waste products.

Injury Prevention

Your body works as a unit. Imagine trying to punch using only your right arm. Not only would your punch be weak and ineffective, you'd likely hurt yourself. A punch involves your whole body—your right arm to punch with, your left arm to provide a counter force, your shoulders and upper back to balance the movements of your arms, your legs to deliver force from the ground, your lower back and hips to transfer that power to the upper body, even your head and neck to keep the force focused rather than dispersing it through poor posture.

If any one of these parts is functioning below par, your punch suffers the effects. Imagine that your back is stiff and sore. How will you transfer the force generated by the large strong muscles in your legs to the smaller muscles in your arms? You might try to compensate by punching from your upper back or arm muscles and ending up with an injured elbow or strained back. By keeping your whole body toned and flexible, you can prevent injuries ranging from aches and pains to serious joint damage.

As a martial artist, you need to prepared not only for the movements you expect to perform, but for the unexpected as well.

Regular movement lubricates and strengthens the muscles, joints and ligaments, leading to improved flexibility. When your body is more flexible, it is better able to respond to the occasional overextension or sudden twisting movement that might happen in the course of sparring, grappling, jumping or bag work. As a martial artist, you need to prepared not only for the movements you expect to perform, but for the unexpected as well.

On a daily basis, stretching can also reduce "day after" muscle soreness. As you age and your body takes longer to recover from workouts, this will increasingly be a gift to your tired muscles.

Focus

Stretching can be a meditative activity. When you stretch, focus not only on loosening your muscles, but on synchronizing your breathing with your movements. Deep breathing enhances your stretches, allowing your body to relax more fully. It also creates a calmness in your mind that enhances concentration and reduces the "chatter" that builds up in your head on a daily basis

Relaxation

Physical tightness is counterproductive to the principles of movement in the martial arts. In order to generate power and speed, you must relax prior to movement and, often, during movements. Stretching not only relaxes individual muscles, it creates an overall feeling of relaxed readiness in your body that allows you to take on the challenges of martial arts with confidence.

Stress Relief

Stress is often manifested in our body as tightness. Stiff neck, sore back, tight hamstrings, chronic headaches and hunched shoulders are all signs of excess stress. By spending ten minutes a day stretching and relaxing problem areas, your overall stress levels will be reduced.

Beginning on page 55, you will find "Shortcuts" to relieving tension in certain areas of the body. If you find yourself especially stressed out, take a few minutes to identify where in your body the stress is accumulating and target it with two or three stretching shortcuts for quick relief.

◎ Stretching Basics

There are four basic components to a good stretching workout:

Alignment

Your body is designed to work in very specific ways. The deeper your understanding of your body's natural workings, the more effective your stretching, conditioning and martial arts training will be.

When stretching, using this knowledge of your body's ideal natural motion is essential. Performing a stretch incorrectly can result in damage to your muscles or, more commonly, your joints or connective tissue. If you have been taught to associate pain with stretching, it's time to change your approach. Stretching should never be painful. During each stretch, you should feel a pulling sensation in the target muscles. You should not feel pain in other muscles or in your joints. For example, if you are doing a quad stretch and feel pain in your knees or a strain on your back, stop immediately and reassess your posture. During a quad stretch, you should only feel a pulling sensation in your quadriceps muscles, nothing more.

For each exercise that you choose to practice from this book, read the instructions and compare your posture to that of the person performing the stretch in the accompanying photos. Some exercises require specific placement of your hands or feet, a straightening or bending of the knees or a particular alignment of the hips or spine. Where noted, pay special attention to these seemingly minor details. Proper alignment ensures that you are hitting the target muscles and truly improving your flexibility.

Stretching should never be painful.

During a quad stretch, for example, you should never feel pain in your knee.

Control

From your martial arts training, you should already be well aware of the need for control in your movements. A controlled punch is much more likely to hit its target than a wild swing. The same principal holds true for stretching. A controlled stretch is much more likely to stretch the target muscle effectively. Before you begin a stretch, have an idea of what your limits are for that exercise. By knowing how far you can safely push yourself, you lessen the risk of injury. A controlled approach to stretching also gives you a benchmark against which to measure your gains. If you know your limits, then you will see clear evidence of your progress as those limits increase.

In addition to controlling the pace of your stretching, you need to carefully control the external parameters. The use of gravity or momentum in stretching can be particularly dangerous. If you suspend yourself between two chairs to force yourself into a deeper split, you are using gravity. If you swing your leg up as high and as hard as you can, you are using momentum to increase the stretch beyond what you would normally be able to achieve. While advanced athletes successfully use both gravity and momentum in their flexibility training, beginning and intermediate level martial artists will find controlled stretching safer and more effective.

When stretching with a partner, you should always be the one in control. Never allow a partner to push you beyond your comfort zone or to apply a stretch to the point of pain. Staying in control of your body throughout each stretch prevents injuries and increases the effectiveness of your stretching routine.

Fluidity

Your muscles prefer flowing movements to jerky or sudden movements. When stretching, fluid movements encourage and allow your muscles to reach their maximum potential.

Fluidity in static stretching means moving into and out of the stretch at a measured and equal pace. Do not bounce during a stretch or try to push out another inch just before you release the stretch. If you feel like you can move deeper into a stretch, complete that repetition and perform another one, going deeper in one controlled movement.

In dynamic stretches, fluid movements reduce the risk of pushing too hard or allowing momentum to take over. Though they allow for movement to extended positions of flexibility, dynamic stretches should never be ballistic (hard, powerful movements). You should feel as though you can comfortably halt at any point in the movement and are never out of control.

Breathing

Deep breathing during stretching has many benefits. It provides you with a rhythm for your stretches. It supplies much needed oxygen to your muscles. It expels waste products from your body. Most importantly, it enhances your level of relaxation both during exercise and afterward.

In general, breathe in prior to a stretch and breathe out as you move into the stretch. Once you have achieved a maximum stretch, breathe freely. Never hold your breath during a stretch.

Once you have achieved a maximum stretch, breathe freely. Never hold your breath during a stretch.

How Stretching Works

Your skeletal muscles are designed to move your body. By contracting (getting shorter) your muscles pull on your bones and create movement. If the muscles and their surrounding tissues (fascia) are elastic, the joint is able to move through its maximum range of motion. If the muscles are tight, the range of motion is limited. Although muscles are generally long enough to accommodate the full range of motion, they are limited in elasticity by the conditioned response of the myotatic reflex.

When a muscle lengthens beyond a certain point, the myotatic reflex causes it to tighten and attempt to shorten. It's a simple process wherein the muscle fibers and spindles register a sudden unexpected increase in their length and fire off a message via the nervous system to contract the affected muscle, thereby stopping the lengthening and potentially heading off a catastrophe that might result in a muscle tear. This is the tension you feel during stretching exercises.

Although it may seem like a hindrance to flexibility, the myotatic reflex is desirable because it prevents, in many cases, muscle strains and tears. Without it your muscles would be allowed to overextend and tear easily. Through stretching, you not only lengthen your muscles, but you reset your myotatic reflex to a higher tolerance.

Reciprocal Inhibition

Reciprocal inhibition can be used to your advantage in stretching. Your skeletal muscles operate in pairs, with one contracting (the agonist) while the opposing muscle relaxes (the antagonist). The function of the agonist is to move the bone or joint while the function of the antagonist is to both allow the movement and to slow it if necessary. For example, when you bend your leg at the knee, the hamstring muscles at the back of your thigh receive a message from the nervous system to contract. The opposing quadriceps muscle at the front of your thigh does not receive a message to contract so it is therefore allowed to relax and lengthen as the leg bends. If the quadriceps contracted or did not relax simultaneous to the contraction of the hamstring, your knee would be unable to bend.

To feel reciprocal inhibition in action, set your hand on a table in the position of a knife hand strike and push downward. With your other hand, feel the triceps muscle in the back of your arm. It should be tensed with the effort of pushing on the table. Now feel how relaxed the antagonist muscle—the biceps—is as it allows the triceps to contract.

The result of this function is that the muscle that is not contracting is inhibited, i.e. its ability to contract is suppressed. This principle can be used to enhance the results of your stretching program by inducing the inhibition response just prior to stretching a muscle. For example,

Through stretching, you not only lengthen your muscles, but you reset your myotatic reflex to a higher tolerance.

when stretching your hamstring muscles in a forward bend, focus on contracting your quadriceps by pulling upward, as if you were pulling your kneecaps up toward your hips. The contraction of your quads signals your hamstrings to release further, allowing you to achieve a deeper stretch. This technique also develops strength in the quads. If you apply this principle to each stretch, you will build both strength and flexibility in opposing pairs of muscles, a nearly perfect model for increasing your flexibility.

◎ Bones, Joints and Connective Tissue

How flexible you are is dependent on more than simply how elastic your muscle tissue is. The contributions of the various components of the joint can be broken down as: the joint capsule including ligaments is the most important factor (47%), followed by the muscles and their fascial sheaths (41%), the tendons (10%), and least importantly the skin (2%) (Johns and Wright, 1962). Although the ligaments and tendons contribute significantly to your degree of flexibility, it would be unwise to target them for stretching with any intensity.

When stretching, if you feel pain within a joint, stop immediately.

A far safer strategy is to target the muscles and their sheaths. The construction of muscle tissue allows it to safely lengthen, whereas the tendons and ligaments are less elastic, making them susceptible to permanent damage. Tendons and ligaments are not only less elastic than muscle tissue, they have a poor blood supply leading to longer healing times or even a complete lack of healing once they are overstretched. If a joint suffers from one or more overstretched ligaments or tendons, it becomes unstable and ripe for further injury. When stretching, if you ever feel pain within a joint, stop immediately. Pain in a joint indicates that you are stretching improperly, stressing the internal structure of the joint rather than the adjoining muscles.

Physical Components of Flexibility	
Ligaments	47%
Muscles & sheaths	41%
Tendons	10%
Skin	2%

Bones and Joints

Your bones and joints set the baseline for your level of flexibility. For example, no matter how hard you might try, you'd never be able to bend your arm backward at the elbow joint without first destroying the construction of the joint. The structure of a normal elbow joint doesn't allow this type of movement. Although some studies have shown that training produced modifications in bone and joint structure in dancers, this isn't a realistic goal for the average martial artist.

Tendons

Tendons are tough inelastic connective tissue that connect muscle to bone. They are not meant to stretch and cannot be elongated more than three to four percent without risking damage to the connecting muscle. Because tendons are stronger than muscle, a sudden overload is more likely to result in damage to the muscle than a rupture of the tendon.

Overly tight muscles, however, can cause unnecessary wear and tear on their associated tendons, resulting in chronic tendon pain. In fact, a skeletal muscle can exert as much as fifty pounds of pull for each square inch of muscle tissue, meaning that large muscles have the potential to generate several thousand pounds of pull, enough to tear a tendon in extreme circumstances.

Maintaining a good range of motion in the body's skeletal muscles can relieve unnecessary stress on the tendons and prevent tendon problems down the road.

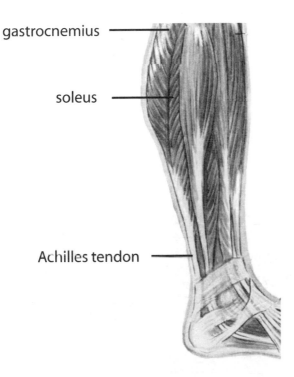

gastrocnemius

soleus

Achilles tendon

Note how the gastrocnemius and soleus muscles become the Achilles tendon at the bottom of the fleshy part of the calf. As you can see, tight calf muscles would inhibit the function of the Achilles tendon and potentially lead to a muscle or tendon injury.

Ligaments

Ligaments connect bone to bone and act as stabilizers within the joints. Their elasticity varies, with the ligaments in the feet and spine being the most elastic and therefore the most susceptible to injury. The elasticity of the ligaments also varies with gender (women tend to have more elastic ligaments), age and fitness level.

While they can stand a tremendous amount of stress for a short period, if a sudden force is not relieved before it exceeds the strength of the ligament, it may partially or fully tear. Once a partial tear occurs, the damage is repaired by the growth of scar tissue, resulting in a permanent elongation of the ligament. Ligaments can also be damaged by repeated stress or overstretching in incorrect positions. Over time, the ligament elongates and the joint is weakened. Any damage to the ligament reduces its effectiveness in stabilizing the joint, potentially leading to repeated injuries to the joint or ligament.

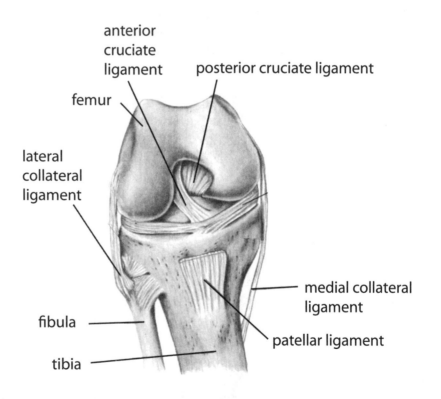

In the above illustration of the knee joint, you can see how a network of ligaments joins the bones of the thigh (femur) and calf (fibula and tibia).

Muscles

The movements of your body are controlled by the contraction and elongation of over six hundred skeletal muscles. There are three types of contractions employed by these muscles:

Concentric Contraction: A concentric contraction takes place when a muscle shortens to move a body part against resistance. For example, when doing a bicep curl, the muscle shortens to lift the weight toward your body.

Eccentric Contraction: An eccentric contraction can be a bit confusing since the muscle is actually lengthening and we tend to think of shortening when we hear the word contraction. During an eccentric contraction, the muscle lengthens under tension, such as when you straighten your arm to set a heavy object down slowly. If your arm's flexor muscles were not actively working to provide resistance while lengthening, the object's weight would cause your arm to lengthen suddenly, much like a weight attached to a bungee cord.

Isometric Contraction: When the tension in a muscle is insufficient to overcome a given resistance, the length of the muscle remains unchanged (neither eccentric nor concentric). Energy is expended but no motion is produced, resulting in an isometric contraction. An example of this is pushing against an immovable object, such as a wall. Your arm muscles can work at full strength, but there is no movement in your arms because the resistance offered by the wall is greater than the strength of your muscles.

Often, muscle contractions are both isometric and isotonic (eccentric/ concentric) during a single movement. For example, when you take a step forward, some muscles contract and relax to bend and straighten your legs while others function isometrically to maintain the stiffness in your leg. If some of your muscles did not contract isotonically to maintain your skeletal structure, your leg would collapse when your foot hit the ground.

Your skeletal muscles are made up of two types of fibers: extrafusal and intrafusal. Extrafusal fibers contain myofibrils, which control the contracting, relaxing and lengthening actions of the muscles. Myofibrils are made up of bands and between the bands are sarcomeres. The sarcomeres contain myofilaments which in turn are made up of two proteins: actin and myosin. The actin and myosin slide over each other, merging to allow the muscle fiber to contract or elongate.

A number of changes take place in your muscles and their surrounding tissue as a result of stretching. Each muscle fiber is made up of hundreds of sarcomeres, the basic contractile unit of the muscle. When a muscle contracts, each of its sarcomeres shorten to bring about the contraction. Studies have shown that over time, stretching can increase the number

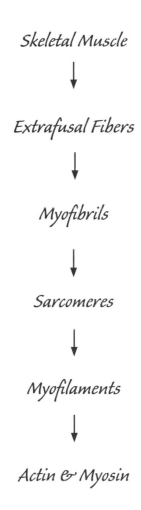

Skeletal Muscle

↓

Extrafusal Fibers

↓

Myofibrils

↓

Sarcomeres

↓

Myofilaments

↓

Actin & Myosin

of sarcomeres, increasing the length of the muscle as well as its capacity for contraction. That would mean an increase in both flexibility and muscle capacity.

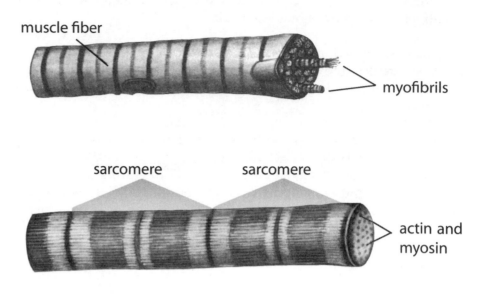

The fascia, the sheaths surrounding the muscle tissue, also increase in length with consistent stretching.

The above is a very general explanation of the way stretching works and probably as much as the average martial artists needs to know to understand how flexibility is increased. If you have a particular interest in muscle physiology, there are many good kinesology books that present detailed explanations of the workings of the muscular system.

◎ Methods of Stretching

Before we look at the most common types of stretching, we should differentiate between stretching and warming up. Many amateur athletes, including martial artists, assume that terms are interchangeable. While you may include light stretching in your warm-up, stretching to increase flexibility should never be a part of warming up. A warm-up is best made up of five to ten minutes of light aerobic activity that engages the whole body. It should increase the body temperature and circulation but not be fatiguing.

Stretching to increase flexibility should ideally be done after the strength and cardio portions of training, when the muscles are at their warmest.

Stretching to increase flexibility should never be a part of warming up

Static Stretching

Static Stretching = lengthening a muscle and then holding it

Static stretching is the process of lengthening a muscle or muscle group to the extent of its range of motion and then holding it while the muscle relaxes. For beginning martial artists, static stretching is recommended as the primary means of increasing flexibility. It carries the least risk of injury and allows for gradual progress and maximum relaxation into the stretch. Since relaxing the muscle is the number one goal of stretching, static stretching allows a beginning martial artist to develop the correct stretching mind set.

Static stretching is also a good rehabilitation tool and you will find many static stretches in this book suitable for re-strengthening and increasing the range of motion in a previously injured body part. The most effective gains in static stretching are generally experienced by holding each stretch for fifteen to twenty seconds for two to four repetitions at each workout.

Static stretching has a number of advantages:

- It is easy to learn and execute, even for people with limited flexibility or athletic experience.

- The risk of injury is low.

- It allows time for relaxation into the stretch which promotes resetting of the stretch (myotatic) reflex.

- It can be done at a variety of degrees of difficulty allowing for controlled rehabilitation of injured areas or advanced stretches in potentially risky positions.

It also has a few disadvantages. Static stretching is not sport specific. For example, you can't really imitate the full range of motion of a roundhouse kick by means of a static stretch. You can stretch in the chambered or extended position, but that still does not approximate the full range of the kick. Static stretching also does not provide the necessary speed for a sport specific stretch. Since muscle tissue contains different structures for measuring length (static length) vs. velocity and length (dynamic length), static stretching runs the risk of developing only the first type. In fact, some studies have shown that static stretching alone can actually impair sport specific flexibility. This is why it is important to include dynamic stretches, such as raising kicks or arm circles, as well as static stretches in your martial arts training.

Passive Stretching

Passive Stretching = the aid of partner or stetching device

Stretches accomplished with the aid of partner or other aid are considered passive. Rehabilitation stretches often use the aid of a towel or belt to achieve a stretch in the lower limbs that cannot be reached with the arms alone. Many martial arts coaches and instructors use partner stretches for variety and to increase communication between students in a class. While they are no more effective than static stretching, they can be more dangerous. When stretching with a partner, trust and communication are essential. Never allow a partner, instructor or coach to push you beyond your comfort point in stretching.

Active Stretching

Active Stretching = performing a stretch unassisted

Stretching performed without an aid is active stretching. For example, if you were to stand straight and raise your leg as high as you can into side kick position without the help of a partner or stretching bar, this is an active stretch. Active stretching is a useful rehabilitative device or a good precursor to dynamic stretching. It develops flexibility in motion without the risks associated with dynamic stretching. It also allows the target muscles to be stretched through the range of motion required for the target activity. For example, slowly raising your leg through the path of a roundhouse kick develops flexibility for the kick while training muscle memory and strengthening the target muscles.

A modified form of active stretching, assisted active stretching, may produce additional gains. In assisted active stretching, the athlete performs the stretch to his maximum unassisted. He is then aided in completing the stretch by a partner or stretching aid (towel or elastic band). This allows for a deeper stretch than the athlete can achieve without assistance.

Ballistic Stretching

Ballistic Stretching = bouncing

Once a popular means of training, ballistic stretching is now considered too risky to be used without the supervision of a knowledgeable trainer. Although sometimes used successfully by athletes, the risks of ballistic stretching outweigh the gains, particularly when the same or better gains can be achieved with PNF or dynamic stretching.

Ballistic stretching uses bouncing, rebounding or rhythmic movements to take advantage of momentum, forcing the muscle into a deeper stretch. In addition to a high risk of injury, ballistic stretching works against the body by repeatedly triggering the stretch reflex, making it difficult for the muscle to adapt to the stretch and elongate over time.

Dynamic Stretching

Dynamic Stretching = controlled movement

Dynamic stretching is like ballistic stretching without the jerky movements. Dynamic stretching takes a controlled approach to movement, using the target muscle through the full range of motion at increasing speeds. For example, you might begin with a slow controlled raising kick working up to a near-full speed execution. Dynamic stretching is best practiced after a warm-up to reduce the risk of injury.

PNF Stretching

PNF Stretching = stretch & contract the muscles

Together, static stretching and proprioceptive neuromuscular facilitation (PNF) stretching are considered the most effective methods of increasing flexibility by many experts. Both rely on the concept of relaxing the muscles into a stretch to increase their length and elasticity.

The concept of PNF stretching was developed in the 1950s by Dr. Herman Kabat as a means of physical therapy for patients suffering from paralysis and muscular disease. Throughout the 70s and 80s, modifications to PNF stretching theories have resulted in several commonly accepted methods.

Two methods that can produce measurable results in your martial arts training are the contract-relax (CR) and contract-relax agonist contract (CRAC) methods. In both methods, the target muscle is first stretched. Then the stretched muscle is gradually contracted to a less than maximum contraction for four to six seconds. This results in an isometric contraction because the muscle cannot really move significantly in its elongated state. The muscle is then relaxed and further stretched to the new maximum. The theory behind the contraction is that it promotes further relaxation of the muscle once it is released, allowing for a deeper stretch than was initially possible. To get the benefit of the contraction, the deepening of the stretch should be initiated as soon as possible after releasing the contraction. If more than a few seconds lapse, the benefit of the contraction is believed to be lost.

The CRAC method takes this sequence one step further, contracting the opposing muscle for four to six seconds. When the opposing muscle is relaxed, the stretch is taken deeper, held and then released. For example, to perform the CRAC sequence during a hamstring stretch, first stretch the hamstring to its maximum then slowly contract the hamstring for four to six seconds. Relax the hamstring, move deeper into the stretch and contract the quads for four to six seconds. Relax the quads and move deeper into the final stretch, hold then relax. The CRAC method has been demonstrated to be a more effective method of increasing range of motion than the CR method.

The CRAC method is based on the concept of reciprocal inhibition discussed earlier. In the above example, the theory assumes that when the quads are contracted, the contraction of the hamstrings is inhibited, thereby allowing the hamstrings to relax further.

The contractions used during PNF stretching should be less than your maximum possible contraction of the muscle. By not pushing the muscle to its maximal contraction, you will experience less soreness and reduce your risk of injury. It will also be easier for your partner to assist in the stretch, particularly if he is not as big or strong as you are.

When performing PNF stretches, give your muscle a short rest between repetitions and never perform PNF stretches more than once a day.

Many of the static stretches in this book can be performed using the PNF methods described here. Because PNF stretching requires detailed hands-on instruction and guidance, PNF stretching variations are not included in the exercise descriptions. If you have never participated in PNF stretching before, a few lessons with a knowledgeable trainer or coach are recommended. Once you understand the PNF technique, you can easily adapt a wide range of static exercises for PNF practice.

Many PNF exercises require a partner and the technique employed is fairly specific, increasing the chances that you may perform the exercises incorrectly. PNF stretching carries a higher risk of injury than static stretching. Even when you are proficient in PNF techniques, always take care when stretching with a partner.

Aided Stretching

Aided Stretching = stretching machines

There are several popular stretching aids often used by martial artists, including many variations of the seated stretching rack and the more traditional standing cable and pulley set-up. If well constructed and used properly, stretching aids can be a useful addition to your workout. Most stretching machines promote flexibility in a limited number of static positions, which as we know from our earlier look at static stretching is not enough to form a complete stretching program.

Before you use a stretching machine, always ensure that it is functioning correctly and that you understand its usage. If the machine is the seated rack type, be certain that the pads pressing on your legs are located in the thigh area or in the thigh and calf area. Pads located only at the calf or ankle put undue stress on the knees.

Never use a stretching machine to push yourself beyond the point you would normally stretch. It's easy to go too far when working with a machine, increasing the potential for injury.

You may also find it useful to use a towel or therapy band (a giant elastic band used in physical therapy exercises) to assist in your stretches. If you find that you cannot reach your toes in a seated toe touch or a single leg raise, wrapping a towel or band around your foot allows you to get the same complete stretch without straining. Bands can also be used to add a resistance element to your flexibility training.

> **Stretching Method Progression**
>
> Begin with **Static Stretching**
> Progress to **Dynamic Stretching**
> Add **PNF Stretching** at advanced levels
> Supplement with **Passive** and/or **Aided Stretching**

Whatever You Do, Don't Cheat

None of the above stretching methods or any of the exercises in this book will have the desired effects if you cheat. You may feel good about getting a little extra out of a stretch by turning out your hip or rounding your back, but you gain nothing from using tricks or cheats in your stretching. The reason cheats work is because they relieve the stretch in the target muscle, allowing you to "stretch" farther. In fact, what you are doing is not stretching the muscle farther, but taking the target muscle out of the equation. If you can stretch a muscle farther by altering your posture or positioning, you are defeating the purpose of the stretch. In some cases, you may even be setting yourself up for an injury by engaging the wrong muscles or straining your joints

If you can stretch a muscle farther by altering your positioning, you are defeating the purpose of the stretch.

For each exercise, pay special attention to the instructions and focus points and understand that you may have to make minor adjustments for your body type. Your best stretching posture may be slightly different from another person's. The difference between adapting a stretch to suit your body and cheating is how the stretch feels. If you feel the stretch in the correct target muscles and you do not have pain in your joints, you've made an acceptable adaptation. If a change in posture lessens the stretch in the target muscles or shifts it to another area of the body, you are probably cheating.

How the Stretch Reflex Works Against You

Stretching too far, too fast or too hard can make your muscles tighter rather than more flexible. When you engage the stretch reflex by stretching too far or too suddenly, your muscles "put on the brakes" by contracting to prevent an injury that might be caused by sudden or excessive lengthening of the muscle. If you push too far into a stretch, bounce during a stretch or try to force a stretch using gravity, a stretching bar or a partner, you will cause your muscles to tighten in response to the stretch reflex, the exact opposite result of what you are trying to achieve through stretching.

◎ Motions of Stretching

There are four fundamental motions that the body makes:

- Linear
- Circular
- Twisting
- Shaking

Depending on the type of joint, each body part has varying levels of range of motion for each type of movement. For example, your arm can move in the linear directions of forward/backward and up/down, it can make a full circle to the front or rear, it can twist about one hundred eighty degrees around it's own axis and it can shake loosely from the shoulder.

Because of the construction of your hip joint, your leg has great range of motion along the linear planes, but much less when it comes to circular or twisting motions.

Your hands and feet have limited motion when it comes to twisting but a wide range in circular and linear movements. Your head, thanks to the versatility of your neck, can do all four quite well.

So how does this variety of movement relate to flexibility? Whether stretching to increase flexibility or prepare for martial arts activities, you should cover the full range of movement types for each major body part. Imagine a baseball pitcher who does only linear stretches. Would he be well prepared for the circular and twisting motions of throwing a ball? Definitely not. Even though he "stretched" before pitching, his stretching would be incomplete and therefore ineffective.

Shaking movements, while not strictly a flexibility exercise, are a good method of warming-up, cooling down and staying active during down time. You'll often see professional boxers shaking their arms before a fight or taekwondo players shaking their legs while waiting in line for target kicking. Shaking relieves tension in the muscles and joints and helps keep them warm during intermittent activities or rest periods.

Depending on what martial art you practice, and at what level, you may not put all of your body parts through every type of motion, but for maintaining a base level of flexibility, going through a full stretch at least once per workout is recommended.

Shaking movements are a good method of warming-up, cooling down and staying active during down time in class.

◎ Why Warm Up?

Some stretching methods advocate stretching or performing dynamic extended range of motion movements without a warm up. While you may be *able to* stretch or kick above your head without first warming up your body, stretching cold is not recommended as a regular workout practice. A warm up performs a number of important functions that will aid not only your stretching, but your entire workout.

The benefits of a warm-up include:

- Increased body temperature
- Increased blood flow to the muscles
- Increased speed of the nervous system
- Decreased muscular tension
- Increased heart rate
- Increased metabolism
- Improved mental preparedness

If you have the chance to enter your workout more prepared and at less risk of injury, why not take it?

A good warm up consists of simple gross motor movements like brisk walking, jogging, cycling, jumping rope, rowing or light calisthenics. You can also include many of the simple flexibility exercises found in this book like hip circles, arm swings, knee circles and neck rotation. During your warm-up avoid static stretches, hard calisthenics and full speed martial arts movements. Aim for a light sweat and increased heart rate, but avoid activity so vigorous that you feel tired after warming up.

During your warm-up avoid static stretches,
hard calisthenics and full speed martial
arts movements.

Chapter Three Q & A

Why do I need to stretch?

In addition to increasing the flexibility of your joints and muscles, stretching improves your overall fitness, body awareness, energy level, focus and ability to relax. It's also an excellent method of relieving stress and preventing or rehabilitating injuries.

Is stretching the same as warming up?

While you may include light stretching in your warm up, stretching to increase flexibility should never be a part of warming up. A warm up is best made up of five to ten minutes of light aerobic activity that engages the whole body. It should increase the body temperature and circulation but not be fatiguing. Stretching to increase flexibility should ideally be done after the strength and cardio portions of training, when the muscles are at their warmest.

What type of stretching should I start with?

If you are new to stretching, begin with static stretching, the safest method for learning the basics of flexibility training and introducing your body to a new way of moving. As you become more experienced, add dynamic and PNF stretching to you training. Aided, passive and assisted stretching can all be used to supplement your flexibility training as necessary.

What is the function of static stretching for martial artists?

Static stretching carries the least risk of injury and allows for gradual progress and maximum relaxation into the stretch. Since relaxing the muscle is the number one goal of stretching, static stretching allows a beginning martial artist to develop the correct stretching mind set. Static stretching is also a good rehabilitation tool.

How long should I hold a static stretch for?

Fifteen to twenty seconds at a time is ideal.

Why is ballistic stretching not recommended?

In addition to a high risk of injury, ballistic stretching works against the body by repeatedly triggering the stretch reflex, making it difficult for the muscle to adapt to the stretch and elongate over time.

What's the difference between ballistic and dynamic stretching?

Dynamic stretching takes a controlled approach to movement, using the target muscle through the full range of motion at increasing speeds, making it a safe alternative to ballistic stretching.

How can I add PNF stretching to my training?

If you have never participated in PNF stretching before, a few lessons with a knowledgeable trainer or coach are recommended. Once you understand the PNF technique, you can easily adapt many of the static exercises in this book for PNF practice.

Why do I have to warm up before stretching?

While you may be *able to* stretch or kick above your head without first warming up your body, stretching cold is not recommended as a regular workout practice. A warm up performs a number of important functions that will aid not only your stretching, but your entire workout.

Chapter
Four

How you use your body is as important to your flexibility as how often you stretch. Using your body correctly can increase the height of your kicks, the speed of your footwork and the power in your punches as well as ensure that you enjoy many years of relatively injury free martial arts practice.

Understanding
your Body

◎ Understanding your Body

How you use your body is as important to your flexibility as how often you stretch. Being able to do a full split does not guarantee that you'll have the flexibility to kick your sparring partner in the head. Static flexibility (the kind required for splits and other stationary stretches) is very different from dynamic flexibility (the kind required for kicks). When it comes to dynamic flexibility, how well you understand your body and how you use it are key factors. Using your body correctly can increase the height of your kicks, the speed of your footwork and the power in your punches as well as ensure that you enjoy many years of relatively injury free martial arts practice.

Posture

If you practice a traditional style, you have probably been drilled on correct posture in your stances from day one. If you practice a more modern style, you may not give much thought to posture. Good posture can increase the power of techniques, allow you to move more freely and prevent injuries, especially to the back. Some basic posture guidelines that lead to more efficient movement:

- Hold your head straight and your chin slightly down.

- Relax your shoulders and push them slightly back, opening the chest.

- Keep your elbows close to your body.

- Avoid both slouching the spine and overly straightening it. When standing, your low back should have a slight inward curve to it.

- Keep the knees straight but not locked when standing fully upright and bent but not beyond ninety degrees when working in a martial arts stance.

Movement

The second element is how you move on your feet. Runners call this their gait, but martial artists have a bit more complex puzzle to decipher. We not only move forward, but also sideways, backward and every direction in between.

A few key points to observe in your martial arts movements:

- When moving in an upright fighting (boxing type) stance, your weight is slightly forward, your toes are "grabbing" the ground and your focus is on staying light on your toes. Avoid standing flat footed or with your weight to the rear in a fight stance.

- When moving in a more classical low stance, the weight should shift to the standing leg, with the body centered over the standing leg, as the moving leg passes under the body and moves forward or backward. Avoid pushing your weight forward or backward and instead focus on shifting and gliding, with an erect spine and head.

- Move symmetrically and with a consistent rhythm. Avoid favoring one leg over the other.

- Take moderate strides, especially when sparring or shadow sparring. Avoid letting your center of gravity shift away from your supporting leg.

- Keep both knees facing forward. When moving in fighting stance it is helpful to squeeze your thighs slightly, keeping your knees from turning out.

- Avoid locking out your knees. Even when standing in fully upright stances, leave some give or slack in your knees and ankles.

- Steady your hips, balancing your weight equally through both legs when standing still. Whether assuming a forward fighting stance (with hips squared forward to your shoulders) or an angular stance (with hips and shoulders angled to the side) keep your hips aligned to your shoulders to prevent back strain.

- Use your arms to assist in your movement. In a conventional fighting stance, your hands are held at chest/shoulder level and your shoulders are relaxed. Use your arms as a counterbalance to your movement. If your shoulders are tensed up around your neck, your fists are clenched too tightly or your arm muscles are not in a relaxed ready position, your arms become "dead weight" rather than aids in your movement.

- Keep your head centered over your center of gravity. Avoid leaning backward when moving forward and vice versa.

- Maintain good posture, with particular attention to moving your body as a unit. Avoid allowing your center of gravity to travel too far away from your foundation, particularly when sliding or hopping or spinning.

Body Mechanics

The third element is how you use your body to accomplish your goals or the science of body mechanics. The body is an amazing but delicate instrument, much like an expensive airplane. It can soar to amazing heights, but one miscalculation and the result could be disastrous.

While whole books could be written on the subject of body mechanics, here are a few simple guidelines:

- The absence of pain is not an indication that the way you are moving is correct. Bouncing around for three rounds of sparring in a slightly awkward stance may not bother you during a class, but you'll feel it in your back, hips or knees the next day.

- Think before you move. Taking a mindful approach to your training can prevent that one wrong move that you regret later. It might seem like a good idea to join the younger kids for a few jumping flip kicks, but consider your skill level and condition first. If you are in doubt about a technique or movement, consult your instructor, try a less strenuous variation or sit out the exercise.

- Use your legs to lessen the load on your back. When executing throws or lifts, use your legs to load the weight and keep your back erect. Never bend from the waist to lift something, especially something as heavy as another person.

- Stagger the position of your feet when lifting or throwing, so that one foot is slightly in front of the other.

- When twisting during a throw or kick, use your legs and arms to move the weight around the axis of your back. Don't twist your back as the primary source of movement.

- Avoid locking out your joints, especially the knees and elbows. Keep your joints "soft" and supple in movement.

◎ The Sum of your Parts

If you've ever been injured, you know that there's no such thing as *just* a back injury or *just* a twisted ankle. When one part of your body is weakened by injury, the rest of your body begins paying the price. If your lower back hurts, you may begin to feel pain in your shoulders, neck or knees because of the way you are carrying your body to compensate for the back pain.

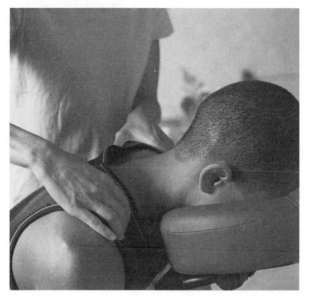

By the same token, how you develop the muscles in your varying body parts can affect how quickly or slowly you progress in your martial arts training. Stretch your legs but neglect your torso and you'll never be able to reach your full potential when it comes to kicking height. Develop your abs but neglect your back and you're setting yourself up for a back injury. Your body parts are interconnected in delicate and sometimes unexpected ways.

Consider the functioning of your muscles during a single body movement. Something as simple as moving your arm directly upward away from your body is primarily controlled by your deltoid muscle (the prime mover) but you don't move your arm by simply signaling your deltoid muscle to contract. In addition to the contraction of the prime mover, other muscles contract to steady the shoulder, making the action of the prime mover more effective. These muscles are called synergists. At the same time, the antagonist muscles must relax to allow the primer mover to work. Imagine trying to lift your arm while the muscles on the underside of your arm remained contracted as well. Your arm would not move. So in addition to developing the deltoid muscle sufficiently, any upward movement of the arm requires relaxation and contraction of associated muscles, and this is just for a simple single directional nonweight-bearing movement. Imagine the complexity of coordination of the muscles involved in something like a jumping spinning kick.

Let's look at some of the ways your muscles, and by extension your body parts, work together to make you a better martial artist.

Back

Your back is an essential energy transfer station. It acts as a direct link between the upper body—head, neck, shoulder and arms—and lower body—hips, legs and feet. No matter what style of martial art you practice, your back plays a central role. If you back is sore or weak, all of your movements suffer.

Some athletes feel immune to back injuries, associating back pain with people who are older or out of shape. Contrary to that perception, back pain is the number one cause of "limited activity" for adults under age forty-five. In fact, after the common cold, back pain is the most common medical complaint in the United States. No one is immune, particularly not those who put increased stress on their back by engaging in demanding movements like high kicks, falls or throws.

Most often, when back pain occurs, it strikes the lower back, the flexible region toward the base of the spine that bears most of the work in our daily lives. The lower back (lumbar region) plays a big part in sitting, bending and lifting. It is susceptible to both traumatic injuries—those resulting from contact or a sudden violent movement, such as a car accident or blow to the back—and overuse injuries—the result of poor posture, repeatedly performing exercises or other movements incorrectly, poor body mechanics or repeated small stresses from lifting or bending on a daily basis. Sometimes it seems impossible to trace the pain to a specific incident.

Back pain, if left untreated, can lead to other nagging aches and pains. If you try to compensate for back pain by favoring or "babying" the offending area, you may find yourself developing sharp shooting pains in your leg or tense knotted muscles in your shoulders. Back pain should be addressed at your earliest opportunity, with a visit to your doctor or a physical therapist.

On the opposite page are suggested exercises for improving the function of your back and getting the most out of this complex, vital region. If your back muscles are tight or you are new to flexibility exercises, select from the Beginning exercises. If you are already actively participating in the martial arts and consider yourself moderately flexible, you have two choices: the moderate Maintaining Back Flexibility exercises or the more challenging Increasing Back Flexibility exercises. If you experience occasional tightness in your back due to stress, fatigue or overuse, try one or more of the Shortcuts.

Back pain is the number one cause of "limited activity" for adults under age forty-five.

Beginning Back Flexibility

Back Shortcuts

Maintaining Back Flexibility

Increasing Back Flexibility

Major Muscles of the Back

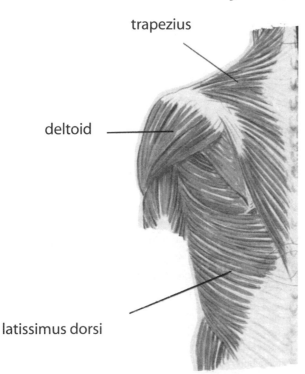

trapezius

deltoid

latissimus dorsi

Latissimus Dorsi: This is a wide, triangular muscle (as a pair, often called the lats.) It extends upward from the lower back, around the side of the torso and into the armpit. It functions primarily to move the upper arm and shoulder in common movements like rowing and swimming.

Neck

If you are a grappler or a full contact fighter, taking care of your neck is essential. The wide range of motion and complex structure of the neck make it vulnerable to injury, particularly from sharp blows to the head, excess weight bearing when on the ground or hard falls. Keeping your neck strong and flexible can prevent injuries and give you an edge in the ring.

No matter what style of martial art you practice, it is recommended that you include at least one or two flexibility exercises for your neck in your warm-up or conditioning routine. Choose from the list below.

Maintaining Neck Flexibility	
Neck Rotation	page 105
Neck Pull	page 106
Shoulder Standing	page 108

sternocleidomastoid

semispinalis capitis

splenius capitis

longissimus capitis

Major Muscles of the Neck

The muscles of the neck are primarily responsible for moving and supporting the head. They include:

Sternocleidomastoid: A long muscle that extends along the side of the neck from the thorax (chest) to the base of the ear. Its functions are to bend the neck forward toward the chest and to raise the sternum (breastbone) to assist in deep breathing.

Splenius Capitis, Semispinalis Capitis, Longissimus Capitis: These are long muscles extending from the head down to the vertebrae in the neck and control movement of the head including rotation, bending, extending and returning the head to an upright position.

Shoulder

The shoulder is one of the most unstable joints in the body, held together not by bones like the hip joint, but by a collection of soft tissue—muscles, ligaments and tendons. This makes it exceptionally flexible in all directions and therefore highly vulnerable to injury. In particular, martial arts activities like punching, joint locks, throws and falls expose the shoulder to a high level of wear and tear. Movements that require the arm to be raised overhead repeatedly or with force, such as a high block or a downward cut with a sword, are the most likely to result in overuse injuries such as tendonitis and rotator cuff tears. Sudden or ongoing shoulder pain should be evaluated by your physician before you continue with your martial arts training.

Because the shoulder is a transfer point for conducting power from the larger muscles of the torso and legs to the smaller muscles of the arms, it plays an important role in a large percentage of martial arts movements.

Below and on the following page are suggested exercises for improving the function of your shoulders and protecting these vulnerable areas. If your shoulder muscles are tight or you are new to flexibility exercises, select from the Beginning exercises. If you are already actively participating in the martial arts and consider yourself moderately flexible, you have two choices: the moderate Maintaining Shoulder Flexibility exercises or the more challenging Increasing Shoulder Flexibility exercises. If you experience occasional tightness in your shoulders and neck region due to stress or fatigue, try one or more of the Shortcuts.

Beginning Shoulder Flexibility

Maintaining Shoulder Flexibility

Increasing Shoulder Flexibility

Shoulder Shortcuts

Beginning Chest Flexibility

Maintaining Chest Flexibility

Major Muscles of the Shoulder and Chest

The muscles of the shoulder and chest primarily function to move the upper arm. The upper arm is one of the most freely moveable body parts because of the structure of the shoulder joint and the web of muscles that connect the shoulder with the upper and lower arm bones.

Trapezius: This is a large triangular muscle in the upper back often referred to as the traps. It connects the base of the skull and the vertebrae to the shoulder. It performs many functions including shrugging the shoulders, pulling the scapula (large wing like bone in the back) toward the spine, pulling the shoulders and scapula downward and pulling the head backward when the shoulders are in a fixed position.

Pectoralis Major: A thick fan shaped muscle of the upper chest, often referred to as the pecs. It extends from the thorax (middle of the chest) through the armpit to the upper arm and functions mainly to rotate the arm forward and across the chest.

Deltoid: This is a thick triangular muscle that covers the shoulder, connecting the clavicle (collar bone) and scapula to the upper arm. It's primary functions are to extend, flex and raise the arm.

Rotators: The Subscapularis, Infraspinatus and Teres Minor function to rotate the upper arm.

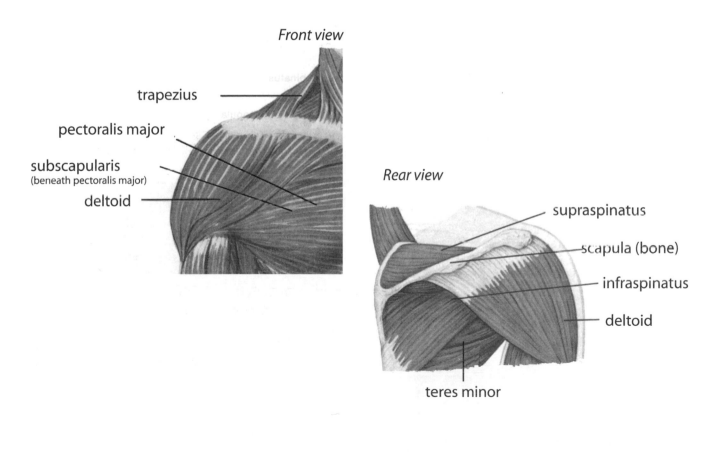

Front view

trapezius

pectoralis major

subscapularis
(beneath pectoralis major)

deltoid

Rear view

supraspinatus

scapula (bone)

infraspinatus

deltoid

teres minor

Arm/Elbow

Whether you practice a grappling, striking or weapon based art, your arms are likely the primary method of engaging the opponent at least fifty percent of the time and maybe as much as ninety to one hundred percent of the time. The good news is that the arms are naturally quite flexible and durable. As long as you are careful not to put unnatural or repetitive stress on the elbow joint, such as locking out punches, it is relatively easy to keep your arms healthy and functioning at peak efficiency.

Many martial artists work hard to increase the strength in their arms, and upper bodies in general, for added power. If you follow an upper body weight training program in addition to your martial arts training, it is doubly important to add flexibility exercises for the arms so that you build strength and range of motion equally.

Always include a good range of flexibility exercises for the arms in your warm-up and/or conditioning program. Choose from the list below.

Front view

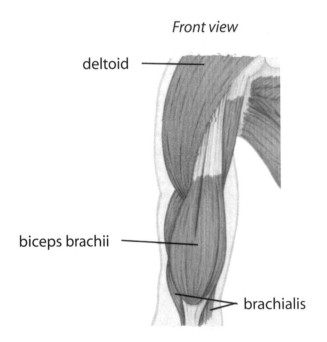

deltoid

biceps brachii

brachialis

Rear view

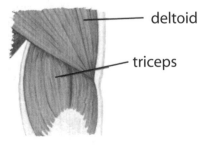

deltoid

triceps

Maintaining Arm Flexibility

Inside Forearm Stretch	*page 143*
Outside Forearm Stretch	*page 144*
Single Arm Twist	*page 145*
Stick Twist	*page 146*
Finger Press	*page 151*

Major Muscles of the Arm

Biceps Brachii: This is a thick muscle on the inside of the upper arm, connecting the scapula with the forearm. It functions to flex the arm at the elbow and to rotate the hand as in turning over a wristlock.

Brachialis and **Brachioradialis**: Muscles that connect the upper arm to the forearm and flex the elbow.

Triceps Brachii: This is the only muscle on the back of the upper arm, connecting the scapula, upper arm and lower arm. It functions to extend the elbow.

Wrist/Hand

The wrist and hand can be a problem area for martial artists. Common injuries often result from poor technique: not making a tight enough fist when striking, not wrapping the hands correctly for bag work or full contact striking, opening the hand when blocking a kick, resisting a joint lock or getting a finger smashed in a stick fighting exchange.

Increasing the flexibility and suppleness in your hands won't save you a smashed finger, but it can help lessen the risk of jamming, spraining or straining your wrist and fingers. If you practice an art like hapkido or aikido where the wrist is a frequent target of attacks and your hands need to be sensitive to the feel of your opponent's body, maintaining flexibility in these areas is essential. Include two to three exercises for each in your warm-up and conditioning routines.

Major Muscles of the Wrist and Hand

There are many muscles responsible for moving the wrist, hand and fingers. They consist primarily of the flexors on the anterior side of the forearm and the extensors on the posterior side of the forearm.

Maintaining Wrist Flexibility

Oustide Forearm Stretch	page 144
Wrist Flex	page 149
Wrist Bend	page 150
Finger Press	page 151
Fist Roll	page 153

Maintaining Hand Flexibility

Inside Forearm Stretch	page 143
Finger Press	page 151
Finger Pull	page 152

Abdomen

While not a major source of concern when it comes to flexibility exercises, the abdomen is a vital area of development for martial arts in general. The abdomen is made up solely of large sheets of muscles, making strength training particularly important for this area.

For full or light contact arts, the abdomen can be a target for punishment by both kicks and punches. A well-toned abdominal area is essential to resisting the cumulative effects of these blows. While knockouts to the body rarely occur, body blows can take their toll over the course of a match, resulting in diminished stamina and power.

Also falling within the abdominal area are the oblique muscles, the wide muscles running up the sides of your torso. These muscles are essential to high kicks, powerful throws and dynamic full body movements. Unlike the more powerful frontal muscles, these muscles can become overly tight and hinder your movements.

Include a variety of flexibility exercises for the obliques in your warm-up and/or conditioning program. Choose from the list below.

Maintaining Abdominal Flexibility

Side Bends	page 155
Seated Torso Twist	page 160
Full Body Arch	page 163
Lying Torso Twist	page 165
Lunging Side Stretch	page 166

Major Muscles of the Abdomen

Unlike the chest and pelvic regions, the muscles of the abdomen are not supported by bones. Instead they form layered sheets that connect the vertebral column and the rib cage to the pelvis.

External Oblique: This is a broad thin sheet of muscle connecting the lower ribs to the pelvis. Contracts the abdominal wall.

Internal Oblique: A large muscle located beneath the external oblique and having the same function.

Transversus Abdominis and **Rectus Abdominis**: These are large horizontal muscles located beneath the obliques in the lower portion of the abdomen and perform much the same function as the obliques.

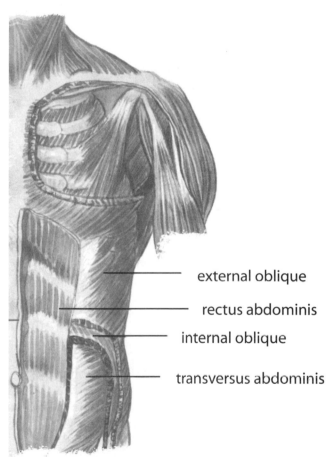

external oblique

rectus abdominis

internal oblique

transversus abdominis

Hip

Martial arts that include a lot of kicking techniques can be tough on the hip joint, especially as you grow older. A number of well-known martial artists have had hip replacement surgery to repair the effects of decades of kicking-related wear and tear.

On a more positive note, the hip is a sturdy joint, much more so than the knee or the back. Because the hip is supported by the large muscles of the thighs and buttocks, it can bear a great deal of strain under normal use. In general, activity benefits rather than damages the hip joint.

In martial arts practice, the hip joint is a transfer point between the back and legs as well as the site of the center of gravity when standing at rest. When striking with the upper body, the hip transfers power from the legs, through the back muscles to the arms. In throws and takedowns, the hip is used to transfer energy from your body to your opponent's and to receive the energy of your opponent's movements. In kicking, the hip stabilizes the body and centers the body weight.

A flexible hip joint increases the height of your kicks, especially the side kick and all types of spinning kicks. It also improves the power in your upper body skills by allowing the lower body to move through a full range of motion when transferring energy from the legs to the upper body.

The pelvis is also the site of the dantien or danjun, located just below the navel, considered the center of the body and the energy powerhouse in many arts.

Below are suggested exercises for improving the flexibility and range of motion in your hip joint. If your hip muscles are tight or you are new to flexibility exercises, select from the Beginning exercises. If you are already actively participating in the martial arts and consider yourself moderately flexible, you have two choices: the moderate Maintaining Hip Flexibility exercises or the more challenging Increasing Hip Flexibility exercises. If you experience occasional tightness in your hip region due to fatigue or overuse, try one or more of the Shortcuts.

Major Muscles of the Hip

Gluteus Maximus: This is the heaviest muscle in the body and covers most of the buttock on the rear of the hip. It connects the base of the vertebral column to the thigh. It functions to straighten the hip when walking or running and raises the body from a seated position.

Gluteus Medius and **Gluteus Minimus**: These muscles lie beneath the gluteus maximus and function to rotate and raise the thigh. They are also known, together with the tensor facsiae latae, as the thigh abductors.

Tensor Fasciae Latae: This muscle connects the ilium (large flared bone of the hip) to the thigh. It functions to rotate, raise and flex the thigh.

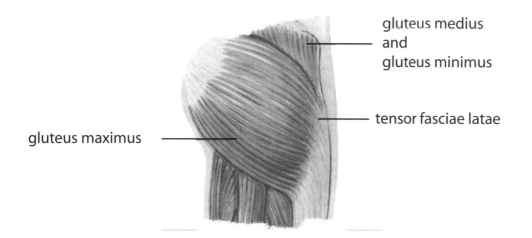

gluteus medius
and
gluteus minimus

tensor fasciae latae

gluteus maximus

Maintaining Hip Flexibility		**Increasing Hip Flexibility**	
Slump	page 182	Cross Legged Side Bend	page 183
Modifed Squats at Bar	page 185	Standing Piriformis	page 184
Partner Groin Stretch	page 186	Advanced Butterfly	page 189
Frog Stretch	page 193	Single Leg Pull	page 191
Cross Knee Pull	page 195		
Partner Piriformis	page 196		

Knees/Legs

Every time your foot hits the ground in a simple walking stride, your knee bears the force of up to one and a half times your body weight. When you run or jump, the impact on your knees is even greater. Squatting puts stress equal to more than seven times your body weight on your knees.

Add to that the low stances, full contact kicks, jumps, spins, lifts, falls, twists and even strikes with the knee practiced in many martial arts and you'll realize how essential it is to take care of your knees. One of the most essential factors in maintaining healthy injury-free knees is your understanding of correct body mechanics. For more details on how to protect your knees when moving in the martial arts, see the Body Mechanics section (page 52).

Keeping the large muscles of the thigh—the hamstrings and quadriceps muscles—strong and flexible should be a primary concern for martial artists of all styles. Even soft styles like tai chi benefit from strong leg muscles, transferring some of the burden of deep stances from the knees to the thigh muscles. If you run as a supplement to your martial arts training, pay special attention to stretching the hamstrings, because runners tend to suffer from tight hamstrings.

A good warm-up of the legs and knees can help prevent both long-term and traumatic injuries. The knee has five major ligaments and a number of tendons, all of which need to be warmed up and lubricated before strenuous exercise.

In addition to the hamstring and quadriceps muscles, the thigh is the site of a frequent problem area—the groin or adductor muscle. If this muscle is overly tight, it is nearly impossible to do a high side kick or spinning kick. A groin pull is a very common injury among beginning and intermediate students, an injury that can linger for months if not cared for properly. Prevention through targeted stretching is highly recommended.

The muscles of the lower leg, the calf muscles, play a substantial role in jumping. If you do a great deal of jump kicking or acrobatics, include calf stretches in your warm-up/conditioning plan to keep your calf muscles from tightening and shortening.

On the opposite page are suggested exercises for improving the flexibility and range of motion in your legs. If your leg muscles are tight or you are new to flexibility exercises, select from the Beginning exercises. If you are already actively participating in the martial arts and consider yourself moderately flexible, you have two choices: the moderate Maintaining Leg Flexibility exercises or the more challenging Increasing Leg Flexibility exercises. If you experience occasional tightness in your legs due to fatigue or overuse, try one or more of the Shortcuts.

Beginning Leg Flexibility

Maintaining Leg Flexibility

Increasing Leg Flexibility

Leg Shortcuts

Major Muscles of the Upper Leg

Muscles in the upper and lower leg together with the hip muscles, combine to create the complex combinations of rotation, flexion, extension, adduction and abduction required for martial arts movements.

Psoas Major and **Iliacus**: These two muscles attach the thigh to the lumbar vertebrae and are the primary flexors of the thigh. They move the leg forward during walking.

Adductor Longus, **Adductor Magnus** and **Gracilis**: This group of muscles is commonly referred to as the thigh adductors and functions to pull the thigh inward toward the opposite leg, flex and extend the leg and rotate the thigh. They connect the pelvis to the thigh.

Biceps Femoris, **Semitendinosus**, and **Semimembranosus**: These three muscles collectively make up the hamstrings running down the back of the thigh, connecting the lower part of the hip bone to the thigh and lower leg. They function to flex, extend and rotate the leg.

Sartorius: This long strap like muscle crosses diagonally over the front of the thigh and across the inner side of the knee. It connects the hip to the lower leg and assists in many movements including flexing and rotating the leg.

Quadriceps Femoris: This large muscle covers the front and sides of the thigh and functions as the primary means of extending the knee/ lower leg.

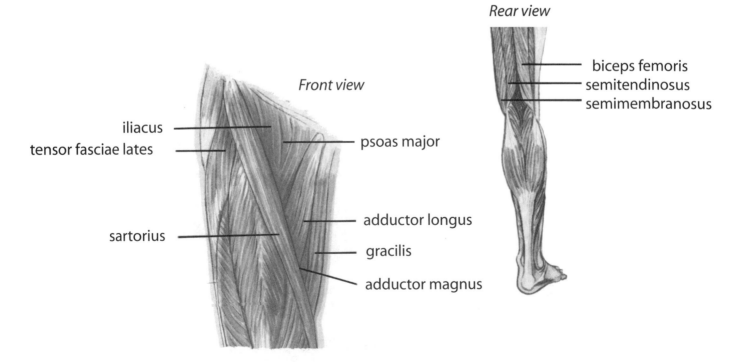

Rear view

biceps femoris
semitendinosus
semimembranosus

Front view

iliacus
tensor fasciae lates

psoas major

sartorius

adductor longus

gracilis

adductor magnus

Major Muscles of the Lower Leg and Foot

Many of the muscles that move the ankle and foot are located in the lower leg.

Tibialis Anterior: This long muscle runs along the front of the shin, attaching the bones of the shin to the bones of the foot and ankle. It functions to move the foot toward the shin and to twist the foot inward.

Peroneus Tertius: This muscle connects the shin to the outside of the foot. It functions to move the foot toward the shin and to twist the foot outward.

Extensor Digitorum Longus: This long muscle runs along the outside of the calf, just behind the tibialis anterior. It connects the shin bones to the foot, terminating in a four part tendon that attaches to each of the four smaller toes. Because of its unique structure, this muscle can move both the foot and the toes.

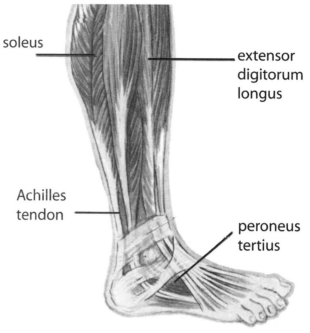

Gastrocnemius: This thick muscle runs down the back of the lower leg, forming part of the fleshy area of the calf. It joins the top of one of the lower leg bones to the heel bone via the Achilles tendon. It functions to flex the leg at the knee and to press the foot away from the shin bone, as in the push-off segment of walking or running movements.

Soleus: A thick flat muscle located beneath the gastrocnemius. Together, these two muscles form the fleshy part of the calf. The soleus is similar in function and location to the gastrocnemius.

Flexor Digitorum Longus: A counterpart of the extensor digitorum longus, this long muscle runs from beneath the soleus, through the ankle and along the bottom of the foot, where it terminates in a four pronged tendon that controls the flexion of the toes and foot and twisting of the foot.

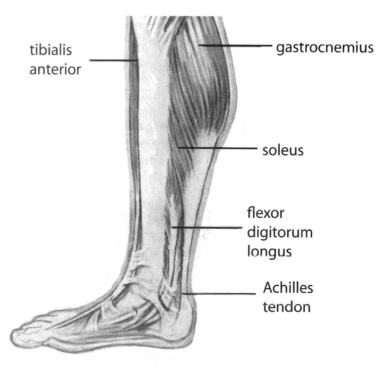

Ankles/Feet

You won't often hear about stretching your feet or ankles, but any martial artist who practices barefoot, should spend a few minutes warming up both feet and ankles before a workout. Because the foot is used for support, mobility and impact in many arts, the ankle needs to be flexible enough to move in all directions, especially under impact. A tense, stiff ankle joint makes kicking less effective and even painful.

Depending on the martial art you practice, select at least one or two appropriate exercises to include in your warm-up routine.

Maintaining Ankle Flexibility

Rest

When it comes to training, you may have discovered that more isn't always better. Strenuous exercise tears down muscle tissue and it is the rest period following exercise that rebuilds and strengthens.

So how much rest do you need to ensure that your stretching exercises are doing the job? After moderate exercise—light stretching, light cardio—a twenty-four hour rest is enough for the average adult. After strenuous exercise—a long run, a heavy sparring session, weight training, PNF stretching—a forty-eight hour rest is recommended before you engage in another session of strenuous exercise. You can, however, follow a strenuous training session with a moderate stretching session the next day. Rest should not be equated with inactivity, but with recovery and rebuilding.

◎ As You Age

In Your 20s

Most people see their late teens or twenties as their athletic peak. If you are in your teens or twenties and in good shape, this is an excellent time to establish good fitness habits for the rest of your life. You may be able to get away with doing less and still excel beyond your older classmates. Because you can, doesn't mean you should.

The way you approach your training in your twenties can determine how many years of martial arts and other strenuous physical activities you'll get out of your body. Make it a habit to warm-up and cool down at every workout, to engage in stretching and strength training regularly and to practice good fitness habits.

One last caution: take care of your joints. A serious knee or shoulder injury at twenty-five can plague you for the rest of your life. While you may feel invincible at this age, your body will quickly tell you otherwise when pushed too far.

In Your 30s

An almost imperceptible decline in strength, muscle mass, metabolism and aerobic capacity begins after you enter your fourth decade. Be prepared to put a stronger emphasis on conditioning, not only to stem the decline, but to prevent injuries. Your body will no longer be as forgiving as it was ten years ago.

You can get the most out of your martial arts training by being prepared. That means taking the time to warm up before working out, spending extra time on strengthening and stretching problem areas, and being aware of the dangers of high impact or hard contact activities. Most of all, listen to your body.

In Your 40s

Many martial artists find that some time after their fortieth birthday, they begin to feel, well, old when they step on the mat. This doesn't have to be the case. You might have a few nagging injuries, you might weigh a few more pounds than you did at twenty-five and you might not be able to fly through the air like the twelve-year-olds in class, but that doesn't mean you can't maintain a solid level of strength, flexibility and skill.

In Your 20s
- *Establish good habits*
- *Warm up & Cool down*
- *Protect your joints*

In Your 30s
- *Emphasize conditioning*
- *Be prepared*
- *Listen to your body*

In Your 40s
- *Build strength*
- *Weight control*
- *Know your limits*

In Your 50s
- *Eat well*
- *Manage medications*
- *Never stop improving*

Put conditioning at the top of your priority list. If the classes you attend are skill focused, this may mean doing additional conditioning workouts on your own. Focus on total body strength and flexibility as well as weight control. Keeping your weight within acceptable limits not only improves your martial arts performance, it means a healthier you overall. Finally, get regular checkups.

In Your 50s and Beyond

Depending on how long you've been a martial artist and how physically fit you've been throughout your life, you may not see much of a change between forty-five and fifty-five or even sixty-five. And if you are a fifty plus adult just getting started in the martial arts, the news is even better. Your body retains the ability to improve strength, flexibility and cardiovascular fitness well into your sixties and seventies.

As you age, you may begin taking medications to control cholesterol, high blood pressure or any number of routine conditions. Discuss the impact of these medications on your training with your physician and follow any guidelines he or she sets out for you. You may also want to see a nutritionist who specializes in older athletes. As a fifty plus athlete, you have special needs, not only to fuel your workouts, but to prevent bone loss and guard against injuries and illness.

A Word About Soreness

The old axiom "no pain, no gain" is only partially true when it comes to increasing your flexibility.

Some day-after soreness in the muscles is normal, especially if you have been pushing yourself beyond your normal limits or trying out new stretches. There are varying theories on the origin of post-exercise muscle soreness including the build-up of waste products and microscopic tearing of the muscle fibers or connective tissues. Whatever the cause, normal day-after soreness disappears naturally within twenty-four to forty-eight hours. Many athletes find that light activity is helpful in reducing day-after muscle soreness.

If you experience continuing pain or increased pain with normal activity, particularly in the joints or near the joints (at the ends of the muscles, where the tendons are located), you may be stretching incorrectly or overstretching. Remember, stretching should never cause joint pain, either during the exercise or in the hours and days following it.

◎ Muscle Recovery

After an exercise session, your muscles go through various stages of recovery, with the most rapid recovery taking place in the first two hours. Let's look at a breakdown:

0 to 30 Minutes after Exercise

- Metabolic rate slows and begins to return to pre-exercise levels

- Heart rate slows and begins to return to a resting rate

- Body temperature drops and begins to return to pre-exercise levels

- Respiratory rate slows and begins to return to a resting rate

- Elevated hormone levels (i.e. testosterone and cortisol) begin to drop

- Muscles begin refueling with ATP and creatine phosphate

- Body begins removing excess lactic acid (waste product of exercise) from the muscles via the bloodstream

30 to 120 Minutes after Exercise

- The body begins rehydrating, restoring fluid volume to pre-exercise levels

- Glycogen stores in the muscles are replenished (this is aided by the presence of carbohydrates, so a high carb sports drink consumed right after the completion of a workout can aid in muscle recovery)

2 to 24 Hours after Exercise

- Carbohydrate replenishment continues, though at a slower rate

- Muscle repair takes place, resulting in the desired adaptation to exercise (this process results in gains in muscle function)

◎ The Right Mind Set

The mind set you bring to your stretching or training sessions can have a substantial impact on your flexibility. Let's look at a few common experiences and see how the mental affects the physical:

Situational Tenseness

Fear and nervousness can make you tense up. When stressed, your body's functions speed up, changing your heart rate, breathing, muscle tension and blood flow. Under stress, your body is prepared to run or fight, not to relax into a split.

Recognizing situational tenseness

Have you ever felt that you were much more flexible when practicing at home than in martial arts class or more flexible in class than at a belt test or a tournament? Are there situations where you find that you cannot perform as well as you normally do?

Overcoming situational tenseness

If you find that your flexibility diminishes in certain situations, some role playing and targeted relaxation exercises can help you relax. First, ask yourself what about the situation bothers you. Are you afraid of failing a test, doing poorly in competition, not being able to keep up in class, looking silly in front of your peers?

Once you've identified the root of the tenseness, begin with visualization. Find a comfortable place where you won't be disturbed, like a favorite chair or your bedroom floor. Lie down or remain seated, whichever you find more comfortable. You can play some quiet music or simply relax in silence. Take a few deep breaths and let go of your everyday thoughts. Once you find your mind has quieted, visualize the situation in which you feel tense. For example, see yourself entering your martial arts school for a promotion test and taking your place on the mat. Be aware of how your body feels. Are you nervous? Be aware of the physical sensations of your nervousness but don't let them escalate into a panicked feeling. Being nervous under stress is normal. Remind yourself that it's okay to feel a few butterflies in your stomach, that just because those nervous feelings are there, they don't have to take over your experience of having a successful promotion test. Take as long as necessary in your visualization to calm your nervousness.

When you are ready, begin to see yourself executing the physical moves of the test. Hear your instructor calling out commands and see yourself responding exactly as you would like to—confidently, calmly and with your very best techniques. Be aware of how your body feels when you are performing at your best and try to associate that feeling with the atmosphere of the promotion test. The more details and feelings you can bring into your visualization, the more likely it is to have an impact on your real world performance. When used consistently, visualization is a powerful tool for decreasing anxiety and improving performance.

Another technique you can use to overcome tension in a specific situation is to try to recreate that situation as closely as possible in a safe environment. If you are planning to compete in a tournament, can you practice in the tournament gym or facility ahead of time? Can your instructor simulate tournament conditions (a ring, judges, referee, spectators) at your school? The old saying "practice makes perfect" applies to our mental skills as much as to our physical skills.

Reducing nervousness and fear can go a long way toward improving your flexibility under "game" conditions.

Temperamental Tenseness

Some people are tense in general. You can see it in the way they walk, stand, speak and even relax. A "tight" approach to life can translate into chronically tense muscles, making flexibility an ongoing struggle.

Recognizing temperamental tenseness

Ask yourself a few questions:

- Do you walk with short, quick steps, even when not in a hurry?

- Do you speak quickly, even in relaxed social situations?

- Do you hurry to finish everyday tasks like reading the newspaper or brushing your teeth?

- Do you often stand with your shoulders hunched up around your neck, your fists clenched or your arms crossed tightly over your chest?

- Do you find it difficult to stretch out on the couch and just relax at the end of the day?

- Do you find change difficult or undesirable?

Many people come into the martial arts after years of inactivity and find stretching the most difficult aspect of practice. They are forever asking how they can become more flexible in kicking or striking without taking a look at the way their body moves through its daily motions. You cannot expect to go through life wound up tightly for twenty-three hours a day and then achieve great flexibility during your one-hour martial arts class.

Overcoming temperamental tenseness

If you see yourself in the questions above, the best place to start your flexibility training is in your daily activities. Slow down when possible. Take time to let your body relax into your physical activities. Be aware of how you feel as you move through the day—walking, eating, showering, driving. Are your neck and jaw muscles tensed? Is your lower back tight? Are your shoulders pulled up toward your ears? Sometimes, simply bringing your attention to specific body parts can cause them to relax, releasing tension that you didn't know existed.

As you go about your daily activities, take periodic timeouts. Spend about sixty seconds focusing on relaxing the major problem areas—the muscles of the face/jaw, neck, shoulders, lower back and hands. Use the shortcut exercises found in this book or any simple relaxation exercises that you like. The focus here is not on improving your flexibility for martial arts, but on getting in touch with your muscles and learning how to consciously relax your body as a whole.

If at first you find it difficult to stay relaxed throughout the day, set aside ten minutes in the morning and ten minutes before bed for light stretching, deep breathing and relaxation exercises. Again, consistency and patience are the keys to improving your relaxation skills and increasing your flexibility.

Conditional Tenseness

Our past experiences can condition us to respond to situations in ways that other people may not. For example, for the victim of a violent mugging and assault, the prospect of sparring or of any contact in a martial arts class might induce tenseness and nervousness. Similarly, if you threw a powerful head high kick at your last promotion test and suddenly found yourself lying on the mat, you might find your hamstrings tensing up at just the thought of having to do that kick at your next test.

Recognizing conditional tenseness

Conditional tenseness can be mistaken for situational tenseness. The difference lies in the trigger. Situational tenseness is a direct result of the current environment. Conditional tenseness is a result of a past experience triggering a reaction to the current environment. Only you can know the cause of your tenseness based on your past experiences.

Overcoming conditional tenseness

Because it is not directly related to the event at hand, conditional tenseness presents some special challenges. You may truly want to succeed in martial arts for the very reason that you find it difficult. If you've been the victim of physical violence, martial arts can make you feel more secure, but it can also feel threatening due to the physical components of the class. Until you become fully comfortable in class, you may want to take private or semi-private lessons. Speak to your instructor about your concerns and ask him or her to work with you in creating an atmosphere in which you can achieve a relaxed performance.

Performance Anxiety

There is such a thing as trying too hard. Every instructor has stories of white belt students who have come into class with so much enthusiasm that they have literally injured themselves by the end of the first class. In martial arts, trying too hard can often translate into kicking and punching too hard, a good way to strain or tear a muscle.

Recognizing performance anxiety

Do you feel that you need to do things right the first time? Do you want to be the best in class or the best at your rank? A healthy competitive attitude is great, but a "win at all costs" mind set can exact a high price on your performance.

Overcoming performance anxiety

First, remind yourself that you're in class to learn and making mistakes is part of learning. Your instructor doesn't expect you to know everything or get it right the first time. Second, shift your benchmark from externally driven goals (to be better than Joe or Mary) to internally driven goals (to be better than yourself of last week or last month). Third, give yourself permission to operate at 90% rather than 120%. Ironically, trying a little less and relaxing a little more will result in a better overall performance. Remember, flexibility is about releasing the tension in your body. If you go at your martial arts training with teeth gritted and face contorted in effort, you are working against yourself.

Self-talk

Loosely related to the above situations is the subject of self-talk. The tapes you play in your head influence your training for good or ill. Tell yourself that you're not flexible or you'll never be as flexible as your instructor and in the end, you'll probably prove yourself right.

Let's look at two white belts on their first day of class to see the best/worst case scenarios when it comes to self-talk:

Joe White Belt: "Look at all those black belts kicking the heavy bag. I'll never be able to do that. I can barely kick the bottom of the bag. I bet they spent hours a day for years to get that flexible. I wasn't even that flexible back in high school."

Bill White Belt: *"Wow, look how high those black belts are kicking. I can barely reach the bottom of the bag now, but I can't wait until I can do that. They must know a lot about flexibility. After class, I think I'll talk to one of them and get some tips about stretching so I can start practicing right away."*

Which one of these white belts do you think is going to make it to black belt? Do you think that Bill knows any more about stretching than Joe or is any more flexible? The only differences in the two are their attitudes and the way they talk themselves into or out of making an effort to improve. Joe is plagued by defeatist self-talk while Bill's self-talk is optimistic and energetic.

You can put self-talk to work for you in all aspects of your training, but especially in your flexibility training, where gains are often slow and hard to measure. Pay attention to what your tapes are saying and reprogram them if necessary. Many martial artists find it helpful to spend a few minutes each day meditating on positive self-talk phrases or to tape a phrase on the bathroom mirror as a reminder.

Why Mind Set Matters

For some readers, the *mental and emotional* side of flexibility strikes an immediate chord, while others have a more difficult time seeing the connection.

"I just want to kick high," you might be saying. "I don't have time for all this mental mumbo jumbo." Depending on how far you want to take your flexibility training or your martial arts training in general, a purely physical approach may work just fine. However, if you want to reach the highest levels of performance, a healthy emotional and mental mind set is essential. Consider the following lists of emotions:

Awareness	Fear
Awakening	Judgment
Curiosity	Shame
Openness	Anger
Tranquility	Nervousness
Energy	Impatience

Which attributes would you rather associate with yourself and your martial arts practice? One of the central tenets of traditional martial arts is the connection between mind and body. If your mind is open, supple and energetic, your body is more likely to be a reflection of that, making ultimate flexibility that much easier to achieve.

Chapter Four Q & A

Why is joint pain a bad sign during stretching?

Pain in a joint indicates that you are stretching improperly, stressing the internal structure of the joint rather than the adjoining muscles.

If a stretch hurts, does that mean that I'm lengthening the muscle?

Stretching should never be painful. You should feel some mild discomfort during the stretch and may have some day-after soreness but pain during a stretch is a sign of pushing yourself too hard.

How long should I wait between workouts?

After moderate exercise—light stretching, light cardio—a twenty-four hour rest is enough for the average adult. After strenuous exercise—a long run, a heavy sparring session, weight training, PNF stretching—a forty-eight hour rest is recommended before you engage in another session of strenuous exercise. You can, however, follow a strenuous training session with a moderate stretching session the next day.

I do mostly kicks, so I just want to stretch my legs. Is that okay?

Developing only one area of your body can be an invitation to injury and will result in uneven progress. While your leg muscles are the primary factors in kicking, the muscles of your back, abdomen and hip play large supporting roles. Neglecting to develop them equally could result in a serious muscle or ligament injury down the road. While you might focus on one area, include general conditioning exercises for your whole body.

How can I prevent training injuries as I get older?

You can get the most out of your martial arts training by being prepared. That means taking the time to warm up before working out, spending extra time on strengthening and stretching problem areas, and being aware of the dangers of high impact or hard contact activities. Put conditioning at the top of your priority list.

How old is too old for increasing my flexibility?

Your body retains the ability to improve strength, flexibility and cardiovascular fitness well into your sixties and seventies.

Chapter
Five

Throughout this book there are lists and summaries to help you choose flexibility exercises for working on certain areas of the body, training for specific martial arts, attaining various levels of flexibility and recovering from a layoff or injury. In addition to these specific suggestions, there are some general rules you can follow in developing a personalized workout plan.

Your Workout
Plan

◎ Choosing Exercises

The exercises you choose can have a substantial impact on the results you achieve. A few tips for choosing the exercises most likely to be effective:

- Choose exercises to target all of the major areas of the body: neck, back, shoulders, chest, arms, wrists, hip, legs and ankles.

- Thoroughly stretch each area. For example, the shoulder moves in multiple directions. Stretch not only to the front and back, but upward and in circles to work a full range of motion.

- Balance your exercises by always working opposing muscles: lower back/abs, triceps/biceps, hamstrings/quadriceps, etc.. Overworking one set of muscles can put you at risk of injury in the opposing muscle group.

- It's acceptable to vary your workout based on how you feel on a given day. If you're feeling especially tight in your back or your hamstrings are suffering from a hard workout the day before, spend a little extra time to relax and stretch the problem area.

- Moderate stretching can be done every time you workout, however you should reserve the more intense exercises for every other day or three days a week to give your body time to recover.

Exercise Order

When choosing the order of exercises for your workout, a mixture of simple rules, common sense and personal preference all come into play. First the rules:

- Always warm up with gross motor exercises (light jogging, bouncing, rope jumping, cycling) before beginning your stretching exercises.

- Begin with large muscles and muscle groups and move to the smaller muscles. For example, begin with the chest and shoulders, then move to the forearm, wrist and fingers.

- If you are doing strength training and/or cardio, do it before your flexibility exercises.

- Work opposing muscles in groups. For example, when working the legs, stretch the hamstrings and then quadriceps, the adductors and then abductors.

Duration

There are a number of ways you can structure the repetitions in your flexibility workout. For more dynamic exercises, like knee raises or

arm circles, between eight and twelve repetitions on each side are adequate. In this book, these exercises are designated as **simple repetitions** and a recommended number of repetitions is given.

For static stretches, two to four repetitions on each side are enough. Begin with a moderate stretch, hold, relax, go a little deeper, hold, relax and continue on that way until you reach your maximum. Breathe steadily and evenly throughout, inhaling as you relax, exhaling as you move deeper into the stretch and breathing comfortably as you hold the stretch. In this book, these exercises are designated as **progressive repetitions**.

◎ Planning your Stretching Program

Your flexibility training is most likely to show results if you have a plan to guide you. How often you stretch and for how long can have a significant impact on your progress. There are varying theories on both and ultimately, you will need to experiment until you find what works best for you. Some common questions martial artists encounter in planning their stretching program are:

How long should I hold static stretches?

Hold static stretches for ten to twenty seconds, doing two to four repetitions on each side. You may want to hold the last repetition for thirty seconds. Studies have shown that there is no added benefit to holding a stretch for longer than thirty seconds.

How many repetitions of dynamic stretches?

Repeat dynamic stretches eight to twelve times on each side, attempting to gradually increase the range of motion with each repetition.

As you progress, increasing to two or three sets of dynamic stretches can be beneficial. If you find that your range of motion is lessening due to fatigue toward the end of a set, reduce the number of sets or repetitions.

How hard should I stretch?

Perform each stretch until you feel tension in the muscle, but not pain.

How often should I stretch?

The average martial artist can benefit from stretching three to six times a week.

When should I stretch?

Stretching can be done at any time after the warm up, but most experts recommend doing flexibility exercises after the strength and cardio portions of training.

Which exercises should I do?

The exercises in this book are labeled for both parts of the body trained and martial arts benefits. First choose a selection of exercises that work all of the major body parts at your current skill level. Include at least one exercise for each of the following areas:

o Neck
o Shoulders
o Upper back
o Chest
o Arms
o Wrists
o Lower back
o Hip and buttocks
o Groin
o Hamstrings
o Quads
o Calves
o Ankles
o Feet

Then add exercises that develop the specific martial arts skills that you are practicing. See the workouts in Chapter 7 for suggested core and specialized exercises.

As you progress in your martial arts training, you can increase the difficulty level of the overall body stretches and increase the number and intensity of the martial arts specific stretches.

What should I do if I stop improving?

Don't expect your gains in flexibility to be consistent, even if you are following a very consistent stretching program. Some days will be better than others and you may even feel like you are backsliding occasionally. As long as you are not experiencing joint pain or chronic muscle pain and you are making progress overall, stick with your plan. If you need additional motivation, revise your plan once a month, dropping some exercises and replacing them with new exercises to work the same areas.

I go to class three days a week. Do I still have to stretch on my own?

If your martial arts class includes stretching exercises, these may or may not be enough to satisfy your daily stretching goals. If you need to do additional stretching, try to fit it in immediately after your class ends, while your body is still warm.

When shouldn't I stretch?

If you are generally healthy and injury free, you can stretch every day if you like. However, any of the following are reasons to check with your doctor or trainer before continuing your stretching program:

o Chronic joint or muscle pain
o Numbness or tingling during or after stretching
o Sharp pain during a stretch
o Joint instability
o A fractured bone, torn/partially torn ligament, tendon or
    muscle
o Recent serious injury or illness
o Pregnancy

◎ Setting Goals

There are three common reasons for not sticking with a fitness program:

- Not setting goals
- Not setting concrete goals
- Not setting realistic goals

Simply having a goal is not enough to ensure progress. As martial artists, we're trained to have goals—both long and short-term—but we're not always taught how to set those goals so that they are effective motivators.

Here are nine tips for setting goals that you can and will achieve:

1. Be specific

For your goal to be achievable, it must be concrete.

Examples of nonspecific goals:

I want to kick high.

I want to do a split.

I want to be flexible.

Examples of specific goals:

I want to do a chest high side kick with my left leg.

I want to reach a 160 degree split on the stretching rack.

I want to be flexible enough to touch my palms to the floor

in a standing toe touch.

Nonspecific goals are discouraging. How will you know when you are kicking high if you haven't defined the meaning of high? You may be tempted to quit early, assuming you've reached your goal, or you may keep raising your idea of high so that your goal is always just out of reach.

By looking at the examples above, you can easily see how the second set of goals is measurable. You will absolutely know when you have achieved your chest high side kick or your 160 degree split. There will be a day when you hit that goal and can feel a sense of reward for your hard work.

Specific goals give you not just the what, but the when of your training. By when do you want to be able to kick your sparring opponent in the chest? By when do you want to be able to nail that head high front kick in your next form? Choose a reasonable time frame for each goal. It may be four weeks or six months, but there should be a time at which you can step back, assess your progress and decide whether or not you've met your goal.

2. Actions vs. Accomplishments

There are two kinds of goals: action goals and accomplishment goals.

Action goals include statements like:

I will stretch ten minutes a day on Monday, Wednesday and Friday.
I will spend five minutes on PNF stretching after each martial arts class.
I will do extra five reps on all hamstring stretches on my left side.

Action goals quantify what you will do, without regard for the outcome, making them very easy to achieve. Five extra minutes of stretching is a simple commitment. It may result in your increasing the height of your front kick, but you're not worried about the outcome. If you have trouble making goals and sticking to them, start with one easy to succeed at action goal, for example ten minutes of static stretching after every martial arts class during the month of May.

Action Goals = WHAT?

Accomplisment goals = HOW?

Accomplishment goals include statements like:

I will be able to kick above the top of the freestanding bag with my right leg roundhouse kick by June 1ˢᵗ.
I will be able to do a bridge within eight weeks.
I will be within six inches of the floor in my straddle split by January 15ᵗʰ.

Because they specify outcomes, but not the process by which to achieve those outcomes, accomplishment goals can be harder to complete. When you set an accomplishment goal, it must be accompanied by a workout plan. What exercises will help you achieve your goal? How often should you do them? What level of progress do you expect to reach in one week, one month, two months? How do you know if you are on track, ahead of or behind schedule?

As you've probably deduced by now, a combination of action and accomplishment goals is necessary. For one accomplishment goal, you might need one, two or a half dozen action goals. For example:

Accomplishment goal:

I will be able to kick above the top of the freestanding bag with my right leg roundhouse kick by June 1ˢᵗ.

Action goals:

1. I will spend five extra minutes a day on groin stretches.

2. I will practice fifty roundhouse kicks a day on the bag, using a piece of masking tape to mark my interim goal height for the week.

3. I will spend five minutes, three times a week on PNF stretches targeting my groin & thigh muscles.

4. I will use visualization during my mediation sessions, with a focus on relaxing my groin and thigh muscles.

The action goals you select are a very personal choice. If you are a beginner, your instructor can help you choose the right action goals to meet your accomplishment goal. As you become more experienced, your understanding of the relationship between action goals and accomplishment goals will improve to the point that creating goals becomes second nature.

3. Multiple Time Lines

If your goal is small and manageable, you'll only need one time line. If it is something that encompasses more than a few weeks time, you can increase your chances at success by breaking it down into interim or mini-goals.

First, choose a target date for completion of your long-term goal. Then create a series of milestones along the way, each no more than four weeks in length, but even closer together if you find you have trouble sticking to a plan without frequent rewards. For example, if you want to reach a 180 degree split, reward yourself for reaching 160, 165, 170 and so on.

4. Focus on yourself

Because martial arts is often a group activity, it can become easy to compare yourself to your classmates, opponents or instructors. For some people, competing with another martial artist, even if it is only in their imagination, can be very motivating. For others, it can be self-defeating.

If you find yourself feeling jealous when a classmate makes a big breakthrough or discouraged that you'll never be as good as your instructor, you probably fall into the latter group. Shifting your goal setting and progress tracking to a more internal yardstick can help you overcome these feelings and rekindle your motivation.

When you set goals, use I/me/my statements. Rather than saying "I want my side kick to be higher than Joe's," try something like, "In four weeks, I want my side kick to be six inches higher it is today." With only yourself to compete against, you have a better chance of succeeding.

Of course if kicking higher than Joe gets you motivated to stretch every day, go for it.

5. Keep a Training Log

You will find a lot of books that have detailed training logs to keep track of everything from how many reps you do to how many calories you burn in a session. If one of these works for you, that's great. If you've been avoiding training logs because you find keeping a detailed log of numbers more of a chore than a motivation, don't despair.

Your training log can be as simple as a single sheet of paper with one column for the date and one for the progress indicator you are tracking. Say your goal is to stretch ten minutes a day. All you need is a sheet like this:

5/9   10 minutes

5/10   8 minutes

5/11   10 minutes

5/12   skipped — sore knee

5/13   10 minutes (upper body only, knee still sore)

5/14   10 minutes — knee feeling better

But what if you're working toward an accomplishment goal? You can still use a similar method. For a kicking height goal, test yourself once a week by kicking a target or bag at a certain height for a number of reps:

5/9   48 inches — 8 reps

5/16   50 inches - 6 reps

5/23   50 inches — 10 reps

5/30   51 inches — 8 reps, 53 inches — 1 rep

Long-term goals are best tracked weekly so that progress is evident and you don't get thrown off your plan by minor daily setbacks.

You can even do both, keep a more detailed training log of your workouts and a single sheet to track progress toward your goal. Sometimes seeing your progress in one compact snapshot is more motivating that looking through pages of training log comments. Use whatever system you find most motivating.

6. Multiple Means

Don't get stuck in a training rut. Pushing toward a goal does not mean you have to do the same thing every day or at every workout. For most areas of the body, there are dozens of stretches that produce similar results. Varying your workout not only keeps it interesting, it brings faster results. Your body works hard to adapt to your training needs. By keeping it guessing with new and varied exercises, you progress much more quickly.

When you look at the exercises presented in this book, many may look similar or produce similar results. In addition to giving you a variety to choose from, this ensures that you won't find yourself doing the same hurdler's stretch every day for the next ten years.

7. Multiple Objectives

Martial artists are natural multi-taskers. In one class, you might practice basic movements, forms, sparring and one or more weapons routines. You engage in individual, partner and group activities that use all of your body parts. Few physical activities require as much versatility as the martial arts. So why not have multiple goals?

When you work toward more than one goal, you not only improve in a number of areas, but you lessen the pressure on yourself to reach a single objective. In a given week, you may find that your leg flexibility is backsliding, but your lower back has never felt better. It's easier to deal with setbacks when you have multiple objectives to focus on.

8. Setbacks

Don't be surprised if you are progressing along nicely toward your goal and suddenly find yourself stuck in one place or even slipping back toward your starting point. Because your body is a fragile, living organism and not a machine, your progress will at times be sporadic or even nonexistent.

There is a long list of physical elements that may lead to a setback including injury, illness, stress, hormones, overtraining, the weather, your diet and how much rest you are getting. When you experience a setback or a plateau, first look at what else is going on in your life. Have you experienced a major life change? Is your daily schedule different than it was when you were progressing? How do you feel in general, physically and mentally? Are you getting enough rest, eating right, sleeping well at night? If you find that non-training factors are to blame, do what you can to correct them or simply resolve to stick to your plan and wait out the stresses in other areas. Even if you cannot keep up your regular martial arts training for a period, try to fit in a few minutes of light stretching each day.

If you cannot trace your setback to a change in your daily life, take a hard look at your training. Are you doing something differently? Should you be? Look not only at your stretching routine, but at your other training habits. Perhaps you've started doing a lot of jumping kicks and your calf muscles are tightening up as they get stronger. Or the time you're putting in with your bo staff is making your back tense. **Once you've identified the source of the problem, a small adjustment in your training plan should get you back on track.**

What if you can't find an obvious cause? Then it may just be a case of plateauing. You have two choices: take a few days off from training to give your body a vacation or try changing your approach. You might switch from PNF stretching to static stretching or shift your emphasis from short stretch times with high reps to longer stretch times at lower reps. Experiment with different strategies, giving a new strategy at least four to six workouts before you make an evaluation. When you're experimenting, keep a detailed log of both your training activities, the results you achieve and how you feel after each workout.

Give a new training strategy 4 -6 workouts before evaluating it.

9. Schedule and Stick to it

All of the above strategies are useless if you don't make the time to carry them out. When it comes to flexibility, you don't need to commit a lot of time, but you do need to commit to at least three to four days a week. The easiest way to do this is to make stretching as much a part of your daily schedule as eating, showering or watching your favorite television program.

Unfortunately, because it's only a few minutes a day, you may find it easy to put off or skip. Rather than promising yourself that you'll find a few minutes to squeeze in here or there each day, schedule a specific time and stick to it. Some people find that scheduling a new habit around an existing habit helps the new habit stick. Tracking your stretching on to the end of your martial arts workout would be ideal. If that doesn't work for you, try to schedule it before a meal, after your evening walk, just after you wake up (as part of a morning meditation is especially refreshing) or as soon as you arrive home from work. Once the activities become paired in your mind, you'll find it hard to skip your stretching.

Supplementary Aids

Stretching doesn't have to be boring or repetitive. It shouldn't be a daily chore that you check off your list, like taking out the trash or doing the laundry. By creating a pleasing, motivational routine around your stretching workout, you will find yourself looking forward to the relaxation and down time that stretching can give you.

Depending on when and where you stretch, you might find the use of supplementary aids helpful. A CD of quiet music, chanting or nature sounds can be a relaxing accompaniment to your stretching routine. Some people prefer to stretch in a favorite room or in a quiet spot outdoors. Others like to incorporate their stretches into a walk around the local park or fitness circuit.

Stretching with a friend or as part of a group can also be very motivating. If you have a stretching partner who is willing to stay ten minutes after your martial arts class, your stretching time will pass quickly and enjoyably.

◎ In the Event of an Injury

At some point in your martial arts training, you'll experience an injury. It may be a minor muscle strain that sidelines you for a few days or it may be a serious joint injury that puts you out of commission for a month or more. Serious injuries should always be examined and treated by your physician. Getting the correct medical advice, treatment and rehabilitation at the time of an injury can prevent chronic problems down the road. Minor injuries that don't clear up in a reasonable period or time, like a nagging groin pull that lingers for weeks, should also be treated by a professional.

For many injuries, your doctor may recommend rest, ice and medication for the pain and swelling followed by a short course of physical therapy exercises. At the time of your initial diagnosis, talk with your doctor about when and in what capacity you can return to your martial arts training. If your doctor is not familiar with martial arts, explain what activities comprise a normal class. You wouldn't want him or her to think that you do an hour of full contact sparring at every class and therefore prescribe weeks off from your training. You may be able to return to limited training sooner than you expect. In general, gentle exercise is helpful rather than harmful to the body after an injury.

For muscle and joint injuries, your physician or physical therapist will give you a set of simple exercises to do each day. No matter how easy the exercises seem, make a commitment to doing them on the schedule that you are given. Your body needs to make a slow, gradual return to activity after an injury. If you already have a stretching plan in place, go over each exercise with your physical trainer to see which ones are okay for you to continue doing during your rehabilitation and which are off limits.

The American Orthopaedic Society for Sports Medicine offers a number of tips for speeding your recovery after a sports injury:

- Maintain year round balanced physical conditioning.
- Make sure that injuries are recognized early and treated promptly.
- Participate in a full functional rehabilitation program.
- Stay fit while injured.
- Keep a positive, upbeat attitude.

Although it's too late to do the first item on that list after an injury, you can begin right now, while you're healthy. The better physical condition you are in, the more quickly you will recover in the event of an injury.

Stretching for Rehabilitation

In general, rehab exercises build strength and range of motion at a very gentle pace through static stretches, aided stretches and resistance exercises using your body's own weight or therapy bands.

Some of the flexibility exercises typically recommended for rehab are:

For the Back:

Side Bend	page 155
Seated Torso Twist	page 160
Back Stretch	page 174
Cat Stretch	page 175
Back Curl	page 177

For the Shoulders:

Arm Circles	page 111
Shoulder Stretch	page 113
Double Arm Pull	page 114
Corner Press	page 115
Rotator Cuff Stretch	page 118
Dip	page 121
Seated Twist	page 124
Stick Lift	page 125
Shoulder Press	page 136

For the Wrist:

Wrist Flex	page 149
Wrist Bend	page 150
Fist Roll	page 153

For the Hip:

Butterfly Stretch	page 188
Prone Hip Rotation	page 192
Cross Knee Pull	page 195
Partner Piriformis	page 196
Abductor Stretch	page 202
V Stretch	page 254

For the Leg or Knee:

For the Ankle:

Although examples of rehabilitation exercises are provided here, you should always consult with a professional trainer or therapist before beginning any type of rehab program after an injury.

Altering your Plan

An injury can feel like a serious setback to your training plan. Suddenly, all of your goals feel impossible to reach in the time frame you had planned and your hard training feels like it's quickly going down the drain. If you are a dedicated athlete, even a few days off can leave you feeling sluggish and discouraged.

The number one weapon you have in recovering from an injury is your positive attitude. Don't get discouraged and don't give up. Most injuries are small bumps on the long road to martial arts mastery.

Your best ally in your recovery is your trainer, therapist, coach or instructor. Work together to set a new plan, one that includes both your rehabilitation exercises and as much of your regular training plan as you can safely include.

Returning to Training

How quickly you can return to your regular training after an injury depends on the severity of the injury, the completeness of your rehab program, how quickly your body heals and your general condition.

During the immediate recovery phase, when pain, bruising or swelling are still present, a course of rest, ice, elevation, compression and anti-inflammatories are generally prescribed. Once the immediate recovery phase is past, you will generally begin general conditioning exercises like cycling, rowing, swimming or resistance training for the uninjured parts of the body. This is an important part of maintaining your general fitness so that you do not fall behind in your training. If you can maintain your overall strength and endurance through crosstraining, your return to martial arts class will be much less difficult. During this phase you will also begin strength and flexibility exercises for your injured area.

The determination of when you can return to your regular martial arts class should be made by your physician or physical therapist, but there are some general guidelines to help you know when you are approaching readiness. A return to class will generally be allowed when you:

- Do not have pain or swelling in the injured area.
- Have regained full range of motion.
- Have regained a sufficient level of strength.
- Can comfortably perform weight-bearing activities.

Long-term Recovery

After an injury, your body is often more susceptible to injury, either to the same area or to another part of the body. Some injuries, like ligament tears or fractures have healing times of six months or longer. Even when you have been cleared to return to class, exercise caution. Test out your abilities progressively, starting at fifty to seventy percent intensity and building back up to your pre-injury intensity over a period of weeks.

Some injuries are caused by a deficit in your conditioning program. Work with your coach, instructor or trainer to create a conditioning program that ensures the injured area will stay strong and flexible after you return to training.

Chapter Five Q & A

Can I stretch every day?

Moderate stretching can be done every time you workout, however you should reserve the more intense exercises for every other day or three days a week to give your body time to recover.

Where in my workout should I include stretching exercises?

If you are doing strength training and/or cardio, do it before your flexibility exercises.

How many repetitions of each stretch should I do?

For dynamic exercises, like knee raises or arm circles, between eight and twelve repetitions on each side are adequate. For static stretches, two to four repetitions on each side are enough.

How I can set goals that really work?

Be specific, have a time line, focus on yourself, keep a record or training log, use a variety of training methods, stick to a schedule and don't get discouraged by setbacks.

I don't have time to keep a training log. Is it really necessary?

While a training log is not necessary to reaching a goal, it can be a great help. Your training log can be as simple as a single sheet of paper with a one line entry per training session.

Stretching every day is too boring. How I can make myself want to do it?

Vary your stretching methods by pairing up with a partner, changing the location or time of your workout or rewarding yourself after stretching.

Chapter
Six

There are no secrets or shortcuts to maximum flexibility, but there are some easy things you can do to get the most out of every stretching session.

the Exercises

Quick Tips

There are no secrets or shortcuts to maximum flexibility, but there are some easy things you can do to get the most out of every stretching session:

- Choose exercises that target the muscles you use in your martial arts movements or with a specific goal in mind. Avoid stretching for the sake of stretching.

- Stretch both sides of the body equally. Many stretches provide directions for one side—repeat the stretch on the other side as well.

- Always warm-up before stretching.

- Stretch daily or at every workout.

- Stretch opposing muscles equally.

- Focus on the muscle(s) being stretched while minimizing movement in the rest of the body.

- When possible, isolate a single muscle group to improve the feedback you receive while stretching.

- Hold each stretch for 15-20 seconds. Holding a stretch beyond 30 seconds does not result in increased gains.

- Inhale prior to a stretch and exhale as you move into the stretch. Breathe evenly and comfortably while holding a stretch.

- Stretch the same muscle in a variety of positions and at a variety of angles.

- Prior to a stretch, focus on relaxing the target muscle.

- Stop if you experience:

    o joint pain
    o sharp or sudden muscular pain
    o dizziness, light-headedness or shortness of breath

- Move into static stretches gradually, maintaining awareness of the muscle group and the amount of tension you are placing on it.

- It is unnecessary to stretch to the point of extreme pain. Once you feel tension, the muscle is being stretched (elongated beyond its current limit). Beyond this point, added tension may inhibit rather than enhance the stretch.

- On competition days, stretch as close to your event as possible to take advantage of the immediate benefits of stretching.

- Know where you should feel tension in each stretch. If you are performing a hamstring stretch and feeling tension in your low back, calf or knee, something is wrong with your positioning.

Safety

There are a number of cautions that should be observed when stretching, no matter how experienced or fit you are.

- The most important rule is to use common sense and listen to your body. Taking an aggressive approach to stretching can do more harm than good. You can't make up for a week of missed practices in one day. Attaining maximum flexibility requires patience. Take a long-term approach and work with your body, not against it.

- If you are uncertain about your readiness for any of the exercises presented here, consult with your physician, trainer, coach or instructor.

- A mild sensation of burning or pulling should be felt in the target muscles when stretching. It should be mildly uncomfortable but never unbearable.

- Wear appropriate clothing—loose fitting workout clothes or your martial arts uniform.

- Practice on a non-skid surface. Many standing stretches require a solid base.

- Stretching barefoot is recommended. If this isn't possible, a pair of flexible martial arts shoes is the next best thing.

- Don't bounce during a stretch. Bouncing causes the muscles to tighten and heightens the risk of injury.

- If an exercise has more than one variation, begin with the easier form and work up to the more advanced versions.

- Focus on relaxing into each stretch rather than pushing yourself.

- Follow instructions for exercises carefully. There are right and wrong ways to stretch every muscle. Good flexibility exercises are designed to provide a maximum stretch with a minimum risk of injury.

- Breathe naturally throughout each stretch. Exhale as you lower into the stretch then maintain an even rhythm. If you feel the need to hold your breath, you're pushing too hard. Instead, relax up out of the stretch slightly and focus on breathing evenly as your muscles release.

- Hold each stretch for about twenty seconds. For some stretches, this might be difficult at first and it's okay to only hold the stretch for as long as you are comfortable. Over time, gradually increase the duration until you work up to twenty seconds.

- Do gravity assisted stretches with caution and only after fully warming up. Gravity assisted stretches are exercises like splits and standing toe touches which use the force of gravity to increase the pressure on the stretch.

- Avoid straining other parts of your body to achieve a stretch. For example, when doing the lying hamstring stretches, take care to keep your head flat on the floor to avoid straining your neck muscles. Cheating to reach a deeper stretch is counterproductive.

- You should never feel pain in your joints during stretching exercises. If you do, stop immediately and discontinue that exercise.

- When doing flexibility exercises that require bending at the waist, always bend from the hip, not the lower back. Maintain a straight spine when bending. The lower back is extremely vulnerable to injuries.

- Stretch both sides of the body equally. Spend the same amount of time on your right hamstring as your left, on your right shoulder as your left, etc.

- Stretch opposing muscles equally—if you stretch the hamstrings, don't forget the quads, if you stretch the back don't neglect the abs.

- Practice slowly and mindfully.

- Pay attention to your entire body, not just the muscles you are stretching. Focus on your overall posture and on balancing the entire body, right and left, upper and lower. If it helps, visualize the physical structure of the stretch in your mind as you perform it.

- Move into and out of each stretch with care.

- Always increase strength and flexibility together.

- Not every exercise in this book is recommended for every person. Physical limitations, preexisting injuries or medical conditions may make some exercises inadvisable. Heed the cautions and discontinue any exercise that causes you pain.

Understanding the Exercise Descriptions

Each exercise description is broken down into several parts:

Primary Benefit

The primary result of the stretch. Exercises are grouped throughout the book by primary target areas, but many exercises stretch more than one area, so a more detailed explanation is provided here.

Martial Arts Application

How this exercise contributes to your martial arts training.

How to Perform

Instructions for performing the exercise. Under this section you may also find variations for beginning or advanced practitioners. Begin with the standard or beginner variation before progressing to an advanced variation.

Repetitions

There are two basic types of flexibility exercises: those performed dynamically for a high number of reps and those performed progressively for a low number of reps. To assist in your planning, each exercise is designated as a simple repetition exercise or a progressive repetition exercise.

Simple repetition exercises should be performed 8 to 12 times on each side.

Progressive repetition exercises should be performed as follows:
- **First rep**: A gentle stretch—just enough to feel the stretch in the target muscles.

- **Second rep**: A deeper stretch—hold and relax into it.

- **Third rep:** A deeper stretch—hold for the longest duration of the three.

- You can perform a **fourth rep**, progressing further into the stretch if you are able.

- **Rest** between reps, either simply relaxing up out of the stretch or alternating sides.

Focus Point

The keys to a correct and successful stretch.

Cautions

Read and follow the cautions for each exercise. The exercises in this book cover a broad skill range and may not be suitable for every athlete. Know your limitations and attempt only those exercises that you feel you can comfortably and safely perform. For every exercise with a caution or limitation, there are other, safer exercises to serve as a substitute.

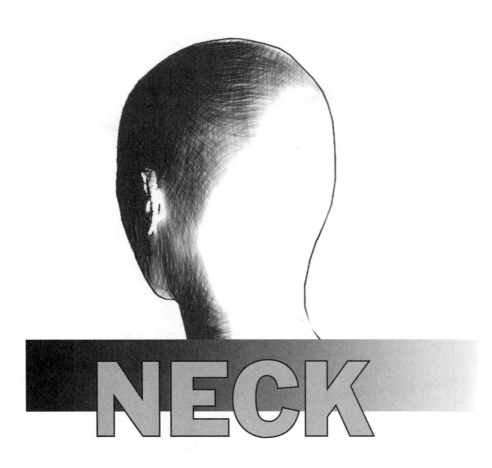

Neck Rotation

Repetitions: 8-12 Simple

Primary Benefit: Prepares the neck muscles for vigorous exercise.

Martial Arts Application: Prepares the neck muscles for falling/ grappling and defensive movements (i.e. bobbing and weaving). Increases flexibility in spotting during turns.

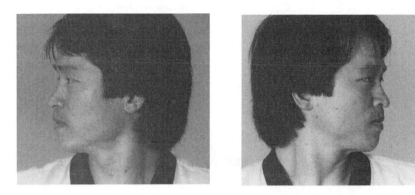

*Focus Point:
Center your neck vertebrae
and execute the exercise
with consistent application
of force throughout.*

How to Perform:

Beginning at the right shoulder, slowly rotate the head down across the chest to the left shoulder and back across the chest to the right shoulder.

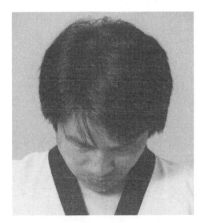

Variation:

1. Look to the left and to the right
2. Look up and down alternately.

Caution: Never rotate the head to the rear because it puts undesirable pressure on the vertebrae. Perform slowly.

Neck Pull

Repetitions: 2-6 Progressive, alternate sides

Primary Benefit: Stretches & strengthens the neck muscles.

Martial Arts Application: Prepares the neck muscles for close combat grappling and resistance movements.

How to Perform:

Place your right hand on the left side of your head and gently pull your head toward your right shoulder.

Focus Point: Focus on a gentle steady pull.

Modified Bridge

Repetitions: 2-4 Progressive

Primary Benefit: Stretches the neck, chest, abdominal, quadriceps and shin muscles.

Martial Arts Application: Strengthens and loosens the neck and torso for falling and grappling.

How to Perform:

1. Lie on your back.

2. Bend your knees and raise your hip up off the floor, holding your ankles for stability or crossing your arms over your chest.

Focus point: Focus on keeping your hip higher than your waist.

Caution: Do not do this exercise if you have a preexisting neck or back injury. If you are uncertain of your neck strength, have a partner spot you by supporting your waist as needed.

Shoulder Standing

Repetitions: 2-4 Progressive

Primary Benefit: Stretches the neck and back.

Martial Arts Application: Helps prevent neck and back injuries in falling and throwing techniques.

How to Perform:

1. Lie on your back.

2. Raise your legs toward the ceiling transferring your weight onto your upper back and shoulders. Place your hands on your hip for support. Once you feel comfortable in this stretch, try placing your palms flat on the floor behind you to increase the difficulty.

Focus point: Focus on aligning your body directly over your shoulders and extending toward your toes. You should feel a lightness in your lower body and a grounded feeling in your upper body.

Caution: Stop if you experience pain in your neck or back, or become dizzy or light-headed. Do not do this exercise if you have a preexisting neck or spinal injury or if you have high blood pressure or are significantly overweight.

Advanced variations:

Focus Point: Focus on maintaining control as you lower your feet, breathing out slowly and relaxing into the stretch.

Variation 1: Lower your legs until your feet touch the floor above your head.

Variation 2: If you need to work up to lowering your feet to the floor, begin by lowering your feet to the seat of chair placed above your head.

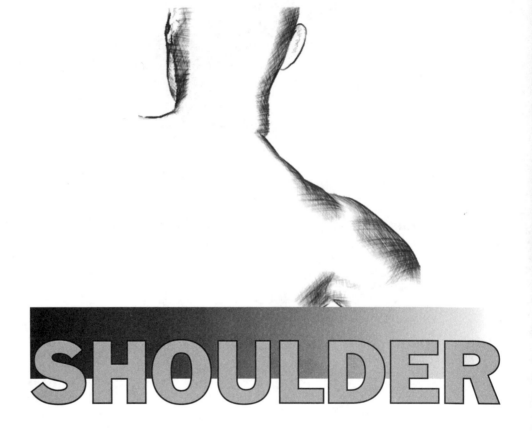

SHOULDER

Arm Circles

Repetitions: 8-12 Simple

Primary Benefit: Stretches the shoulders, chest and upper back.

Martial Arts Application: Improves circular striking, blocking and throwing techniques.

How to Perform:

1. Stretch both arms out to the side.

Focus Point: Focus on tightening your stomach muscles to anchor your body during the movement.

2. Rotate them in large circles to the front.
3. Reverse and rotate to the rear.

Variation:
1. Rotate in small circles to the front.
2. Reverse and rotate in small circles to the rear.

Half Windmills

Repetitions: 8-12 Simple

Primary Benefit: Stretches the shoulder, chest and triceps muscles.

Martial Arts Application: Improves flexibility for striking and throwing skills that require moving your arms in different directions.

How to Perform:

Focus Point: Focus on both hands breaking the plane of your body equally to the rear.

1. Stretch one arm over your head and let the other hang at your side.

2. Simultaneously thrust both arms to the rear twice.

3. Switch arms and repeat.

Harder **Variation:**

To intensify the stretch, perform in front stance, alternating right and left stances for an equal number of reps.

Shoulder Stretch

2-3 Progressive, alternate sides

Primary Benefit: Stretches the shoulders, triceps and oblique muscles.

Martial Arts Application: Reduces the risk of shoulder injury in locking and falling applications. Improves range of motion for punching and other hand skills.

How to Perform:

1. Put your left hand over your right shoulder and press your left elbow with your right hand.

2. Raise your left arm above your head and bend at the elbow. Press down on your elbow with your right hand.

Focus Point: Focus on keeping your bent arm parallel (#1) or perpendicular (#2-3) to the floor.

3. Grasp your right hand and pull to the left with your left hand.

Double Arm Pull

2-3 Progressive, alternate sides

Primary Benefit: Stretches the shoulder, triceps and oblique muscles.

Martial Arts Application: Improves flexibility for striking and grappling.

How to Perform:

1. Hold a towel or belt in one hand and drop it over your shoulder behind you so it hangs along your spine.

2. With your other hand, reach up and grasp the other end of the belt in front of your spine.

3. First, pull upward with your upper hand and hold.

4. Then pull downward with your lower hand and hold.

5. Perform on the other side by reversing the position of your hands. Keep your stomach muscles firm and your spine straight throughout.

Focus point: Focus on a balanced stretch in both shoulders. Do not twist your torso to increase the stretch.

Corner Press

2-4 Progressive

Primary Benefit: Stretches the muscles of the chest, shoulders and inner arms.

Martial Arts Application: Increases flexibility for rear striking and weapons (i.e. nunchaku) techniques.

How to Perform:

Focus Points: Focus on pressing your whole body forward to intensify the stretch.

1. Stand facing a corner of the room with your feet together pointing directly into the corner.

2. Raise your arms to shoulder level with your elbows bent at a ninety-degree angle.

3. Place your hands flat on the wall with your fingers pointing toward the ceiling.

4. Lean into the corner, pressing your hips slightly forward.

Rear Arm Stretch

2-4 Progressive

Primary Benefit: Stretches the muscles of the shoulders, arms and lower/mid back.

Martial Arts Application: Improves your ability to endure joint lock techniques due to increased range of motion (defensive endurance).

How to Perform:

1. Stretch both arms behind your back and interlock your fingers with your thumbs pointing to the ground.

2. Bend at the waist and raise your arms toward the ceiling.

Focus Point: Focus on pulling your elbows inward, toward each other.

Cautions: Do not do this exercise if you have a previous shoulder injury, especially a shoulder dislocation.

Arm Raises

8-12 Simple, alternate sides

Primary Benefit: Stretches the muscles of the neck, shoulders, arms and torso.

Martial Arts Application: Improves flexibility for throwing, striking skills and spinning/rotating techniques.

How to Perform:

1. Stand with your feet a bit more than shoulder width apart and your fists touching the ground.

Focus Point: Focus on keeping your arms on one plane when extending one overhead.

2. Extend your right arm up above your back while keeping your left fist on the ground. Look at your upraised fist.

Rotator Cuff Stretch

2-4 Progressive, alternate sides

Primary Benefit: Stretches the shoulders.

Martial Arts Application: Reduces the risk of injury in striking, grappling and weapon practice.

How to Perform:

1. Stand facing your partner.

2. Raise your arm to shoulder height and bend it at the elbow, keeping your arm on one plane.

3. You partner places one hand under your biceps for support and grasps your wrist with her other hand.

Focus Point: Focus on a slow, gentle stretch while maintaining the position of your upper arm. Communicate the level of intensity of the stretch with your partner to prevent injuries.

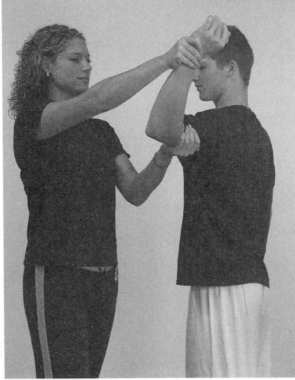

4. When you are ready, your partner rotates your forearm backward by pushing your wrist while maintaining the position of your upper arm.

Rear Palm Press

2-4 Progressive

Primary Benefit: Stretches the shoulder, arm, wrist and hand muscles.

Martial Arts Application: Increases flexibility for striking and weapons techniques.

How to Perform:

1. Standing, place your hands behind your back, palms together, fingers pointing downward.

2. Slowly rotate your hands inward toward your back until your fingers are pointing toward the ceiling.

3. If you are not feeling a stretch, press your palms together more firmly and pull your elbows back and inward.

Focus Point: Focus on relaxing your shoulders and opening your chest.

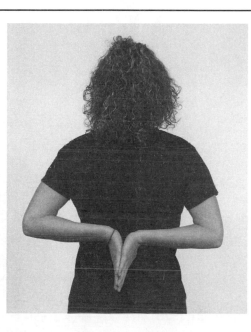

Easier

Caution: Do not attempt the rear palm press if you have had a shoulder injury or shoulder pain in the past.

If you cannot turn your hands inward, simply press your palms together with your fingers pointing downward.

Rear Towel Stretch

2-4 Progressive, alternate sides

Primary Benefit: Stretches the shoulder, arms and wrists.

Martial Arts Application: Increases flexibility for striking, grappling, and joint locks.

How to Perform:

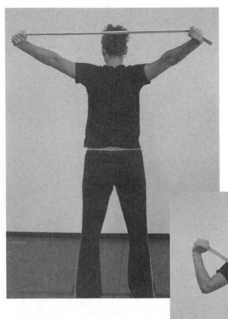

Focus Point: Be flexible in adjusting the width of your arms according to your flexibility level but focus on keeping one arm straight throughout.

1. Raise your arms above your head and grasp a belt or towel at a width of about one and half times your shoulder width.

2. Lower your arms. As you reach shoulder level, bend your right arm at the elbow, while keeping your left arm straight and continuing to lower your arms. You should feel the stretch in your left arm at this point.

3. Continue lowering your arms, straightening your left arm at the first comfortable point below shoulder level.

4. Finish at waist level with both arms straight.

Caution: Discontinue this exercise if you experience shoulder pain.

Dip

2-4 Progressive

Primary Benefit: Stretches the shoulders, chest and upper arms.

Martial Arts Application: Improves flexibility and strength for striking, grappling and weapons techniques.

How to Perform:

1. Stand about three feet from a sturdy chair or stretching bar.

2. With your back to the chair, place your palms on the top of the seatback and bend your knees and elbows, lowering yourself as close to a sitting position as possible. Do not go below a ninety degree knee bend. To increase the stretch, move your feet away from the chair.

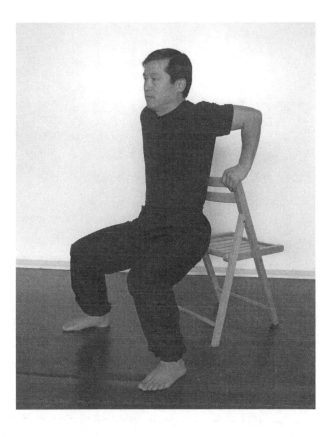

Focus Point: Begin from a static stretch and gradually dip further to intensify the effect of the stretch.

Kneeling Reach

2-4 Progressive

Primary Benefit: Stretches the shoulders and chest.

Martial Arts Application: Increases flexibility in the upper chest and shoulders for grappling and throwing.

How to Perform:

1. Kneel on the floor facing a chair or other low sturdy surface.

2. Stretch your arms over your head and fold them so your forearms are touching.

3. Bend forward at the waist and rest your folded arms on the seat of the chair.

Focus Point: Relax your torso and gently exhale to increase the stretch.

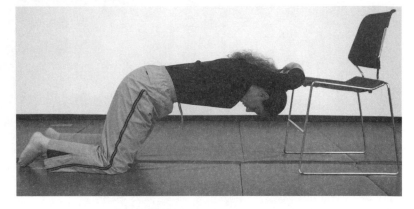

Caution: Do not perform the kneeling reach if you experience shoulder pain or if you have a preexisting shoulder injury.

Kneeling Forearm Stretch   *2-4 Progressive*

Primary Benefit: Stretches the forearms, wrists and shoulders.

Martial Arts Application: Increases flexibility in the lower arm for weapons applications and grappling skills like wrist locks and arm bars.

How to Perform:

1. Kneel on the floor with your fingers pointed toward you and your thumbs pointed outward.

2. Keeping your palms flat, lean backward, lowering your hips toward your feet until you feel a stretch in your forearms and wrists.

Focus Point: Move your entire body backward to gradually increase the stretch in the wrists.

Seated Twist

2-4 Progressive, alternate sides

Primary Benefit: Stretches the front of the shoulders and the obliques.

Martial Arts Application: Prepares the shoulders for striking, weapons and joint lock (defensive) techniques.

How to Perform:

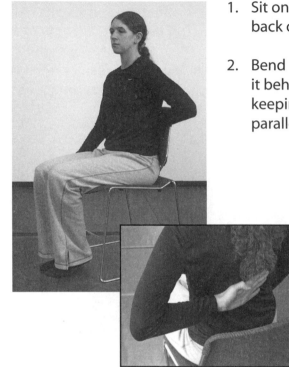

1. Sit on a chair with a firm back or against a wall.

2. Bend one arm and place it behind your back, keeping your forearm parallel to the floor.

Focus Point: Keep your torso straight and rotate around your erect spine.

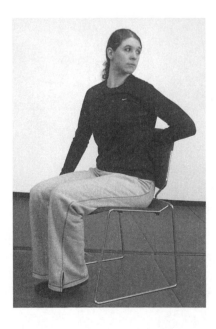

3. Turn your head and torso toward your bent arm.

Stick Lift

10-12 Simple

Primary Benefit: Stretches the chest, shoulder and oblique muscles.

Martial Arts Application: Increases flexibility for striking and weapons techniques.

How to Perform:

1. Seated, clasp a stick with your hands slightly wider than shoulder width apart.

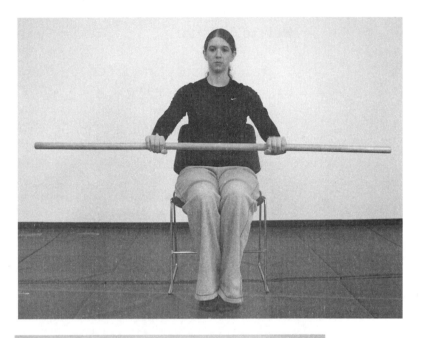

2. Keeping your stomach pulled in and your back straight, raise the stick as far above your head and behind you as you can.

Focus Point: Keep your arms straight throughout the exercise but don't lock out your elbows.

Hand Stand

2-3 Progressive

Primary Benefit: Stretches and strengthens the shoulders, abdominal and back muscles, and wrists.

Martial Arts Application: Improves flexibility, strength and sensitivity to posture and balance in movements that require inversion, such as falling and flipping.

How to Perform:

1. Place your palms flat on the ground and raise your legs up toward the ceiling.

2. Balance on your hands for up to one minute.

Focus Point: Focus on using your total body musculature to raise yourself into position rather than kicking up or throwing your body upward.

Caution: Falling over backwards during a handstand could result in serious neck and spine injuries. Always use a spotter or support. If you have high blood pressure, avoid inverted stretches such as the hand stand.

Beginner Variation 1: If you cannot balance, have a partner catch and hold your legs or use a wall for support.

Beginner Variation 2: If you cannot extend into the stretch fully, balance the soles of your feet on a wall.

Partner Bridge

2-4 Progressive

Primary Benefit: Stretches the shoulders, chest, back and legs.

Martial Arts Application: Increases flexibility and strength in the upper chest and shoulders for grappling and throwing.

How to Perform:

Focus Point: Lean toward your partner to equalize the distribution of force. Cooperation is a must.

1. Face a partner and place your hands on each other's shoulders.

2. Each person takes one big step backward and bends at the waist.

3. Continue moving backward until you both feel a comfortable stretch in your shoulders. If one person is more flexible than the other, stop moving backward before the less flexible partner becomes uncomfortable.

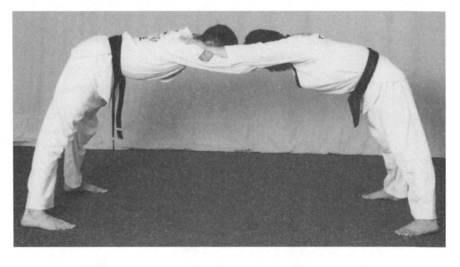

Caution: Do not perform the partner bridge if you experience shoulder pain or if you have a preexisting shoulder injury.

Scissor Swing

10-12 Simple, alternate sides

Primary Benefit: Stretches the shoulders, chest, back and legs.

Martial Arts Application: A good warm-up for movements that utilize the upper and lower body in opposing directions.

How to Perform:

1. Stand beside a sturdy chair or stretching bar and place your right hand on it for support. Raise your left leg to the front while swinging your left arm to the rear.

2. Once your arm and leg reach their maximum height, reverse direction, swinging your leg to the rear while your arm comes up and foward.

Focus Point: Focus on a relaxed coordination of your arm leg. Smoothness is more important than height.

CHEST

Press, Press, Fling

8-12 Simple

Primary Benefit: Stretches shoulder, arm & chest muscles.

Martial Arts Application: Good warm-up for striking and throwing.

How to Perform:

Focus Point: Relax and develop a rhythm.

1. Stand with your arms outstretched in front of you.

2. Thrust your elbows to the rear two times.

4. Return to Position 1 after each step.

3. Swing your arms to the rear once.

Criss Cross

8-12 Simple

Primary Benefit: Stretches the chest, shoulder and back muscles.

Martial Arts Application: Good warm-up for striking and grappling.

How to Perform:

1. Stretch both arms in front of you.

2. Cross your arms right over left, then left over right, then right over left again.

Focus Point: Begin from a small motion and increase range of motion as you warm up.

3. Thrust both arms to the rear.

Up Back Over

8-12 Simple

Primary Benefit: Stretches the shoulders and chest.

Martial Arts Application: Improves flexibility for throwing and takedown skills that use both arms together.

How to Perform:

1. Swing your arms up.

2. Swing your arms down to the rear.

3. Swing your arms over your head in a circle to the rear.

Focus Point: Begin slowly and increase speed as you warm up.

Seated Chest Opening

2-4 Progressive, alternate

Primary Benefit: Stretches the muscles of the upper torso, including the obliques, chest, shoulders and neck, as well as the legs.

Martial Arts Application: Improves flexibility for turning and spinning movements.

How to Perform:

1. Sit with both legs split comfortably to the sides, but not to their maximum stretch.

2. Reach for your right foot with your right hand. Rest your left hand on your left thigh.

3. Slowly twist your upper body to look upward over your left shoulder.

4. Relax your left shoulder backward, fully opening your chest.

Focus Points: Lean your body slightly forward
and toward your outstretched arm.

Chest Pull

2-4 Progressive

Primary Benefit: Stretches the chest and shoulder muscles.

Martial Arts Application: Increases flexibility for striking, grappling and weapons techniques.

How to Perform:

1. Sit on the floor with your legs extended in front of you and your arms out to the sides.

2. Your partner stands behind you with one shin bracing your lower back while she grasps your forearms.

3. When you are ready, she pulls your arms back toward her, opening your chest.

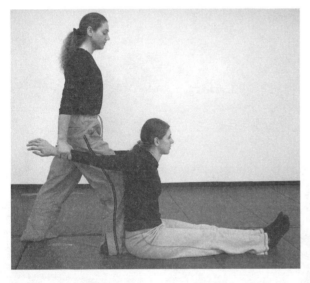

4. Then she releases the stretch and pulls back and slightly upward.

Focus Point: Relax your arms, hands and neck.

Caution: Your arms should not be pulled closer together than your partner's hips and you should never stretch far enough for your arms to touch behind you. If you have ever dislocated a shoulder or feel pain in your shoulders when stretching, do not perform this stretch.

Shoulder Press

8-10 Simple

Primary Benefit: Stretches the muscles in the chest and shoulders.

Martial Arts Application: Improves flexibility for grappling and defensive hand skills.

How to Perform:

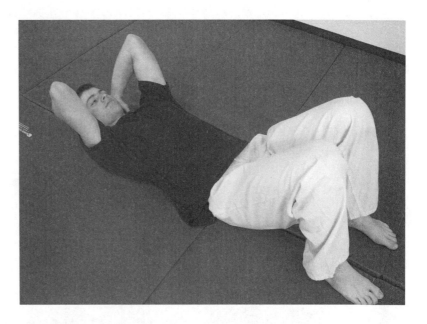

1. Lie on your back with your knees bent and your hands over your ears.

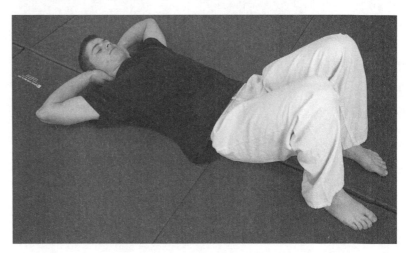

2. Press your elbows to the floor, opening your chest and shoulders.

Focus Point: For the best stretch, your hands should be directly behind your ears when you lower your arms.

Chest Opening

2-4 Progressive

Primary Benefit: Stretches the muscles in the neck, shoulders, chest, abdominal and spinal areas.

Martial Arts Application: Improves strength and flexibility for grappling and striking.

How to Perform:

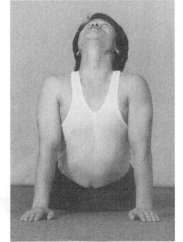

Focus Point: For a deeper stretch of the lower back, press your hip and feet down into the floor.

1. Lie on your stomach with your hands in push-up position.

2. Push your upper body off the ground and fully extend your arms while looking upward.

Harder

Advanced variation:

1. Lie on your stomach and grasp your ankles.

2. Lift your knees and head, drawing them toward each other as you pull your feet up and toward you.

Inverse Chest Opening

2-4 Progressive

Primary Benefit: Stretches the muscles in the chest, shoulders and arms while strengthening the arms.

Martial Arts Application: Improves flexibility for movement on the ground.

How to Perform:

1. Sit with your legs extended in front of you, your hands behind you and your palms on the floor.

2. Lift your torso, shifting your weight onto your feet and hands while looking upward.

Focus Point: Focus on keeping your torso straight.

Beginner variation:

Instead of extending your legs outward, bend your knees and put your feet flat on the floor.

Advanced variation:

1. From the Beginner Variation position, raise your left leg slowly off the floor to about chest level.

2. Lower your left leg and repeat with your right.

Lateral Chest Opening

2-4 Progressive, alternate

Primary Benefit: Stretches the shoulders, chest and the oblique muscles of the torso, while strengthening the arms.

Martial Arts Application: Improves flexibility and strength for grappling and kicking, especially back kick and side kick.

How to Perform:

1. Lie on your stomach and place both palms on the floor.
2. Press upward, looking up over your right shoulder.

Focus Point: Focus on keeping your feet, knees, hip, shoulders and head on one line.

Advanced variation:

1. Lie on your stomach and place both palms on the floor.

2. Press upward, looking up over your right shoulder.

3. When you feel stable, reach your right hand up toward the ceiling, extending your fingertips for a full stretch.

Back Lift

1-3 Progressive

Primary Benefit: Loosens the spine and chest.

Martial Arts Application: Improves flexibility for kicking, grappling and throwing while increasing leg strength.

How to Perform:

1. Stand back to back with a partner and lock your arms at the elbow.

2. One partner leans forward, lifting the other onto his back. Do not lock out your knees when lifting.

Focus Point: Totally relax your body and trust your partner.

Caution: Always do this exercise with a partner of similar weight and height. Load the person slowly onto your back. Do not do this exercise if you have preexisting back or knee injuries.

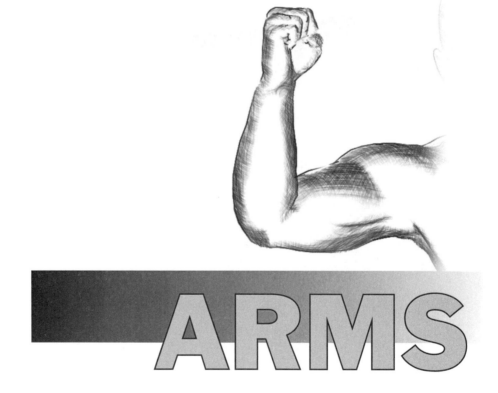

ARMS

Inside Forearm Stretch

2-4 Progressive, alternate sides

Primary Benefit: Stretches the underside of the forearm, wrist and fingers.

Martial Arts Application: Warm-up and conditioning for joint locking practice and snapping strikes like backfist.

How to Perform:

1. Grasp the fingers of your right hand with your left hand and pull toward you (right palm facing away from you).

Focus Point: Maintain constant pressure and wrist/hand structure.

2. Slowly raise the height of your arm to your head height.

3. Slowly lower to belt level.

Outside Forearm Stretch

3-6 Simple, alternate

Primary Benefit: Stretches the outside of the forearm, wrist and fingers.

Martial Arts Application: Warm-up and conditioning for joint locking practice.

How to Perform:

1. Grasp your left hand with your right hand, placing your right thumb against the back of your left hand.

2. Twist your right hand counterclockwise by pushing with your right thumb and pulling with your right fingers.

Focus Point: Grab your wrist firmly but leave the index finger of your gripping hand free.

Advanced Variation:

To intensify the stretch rotate your upper body slowly to the right then left, as if applying a wrist lock to yourself.

Harder

Single Arm Twist

2-4 Progressive, alternate sides

Primary Benefit: Stretches the front of the upper arm and shoulders.

Martial Arts Application: Warm-up and conditioning for joint locking, grappling and striking.

How to Perform:

1. Stand with your left side to a wall and reach back to place your left palm on the wall.

2. Place your right arm behind you and turn to your right, reaching your right hand toward the wall and looking over your right shoulder toward your left hand.

Focus Point:
Exhale as you twist.

Stick Twist

10-12 Simple, alternate sides

Primary Benefit: Loosens and strengthens the muscles of the wrist and forearm.

Martial Arts Application: Warm-up and conditioning for joint locking, weapons and striking practice. Also improves grip strength.

How to Perform:

1. Grasp a short stick (about the length of your arm) in the middle.

2. With your arm extended at shoulder height, twist your arm to the right and left, maintaining control of the stick.

Focus Point: Focus on keeping your arm height level at the center of the rotation.

WRIST

Wrist Flex

8-10 Simple, alternate sides

Primary Benefit: Stretches the top and bottom of the wrist.

Martial Arts Application: Warm-up and conditioning for joint locking, striking and weapons practice.

How to Perform:

1. Grasp your right hand with your left hand.
2. Pull toward your chest.

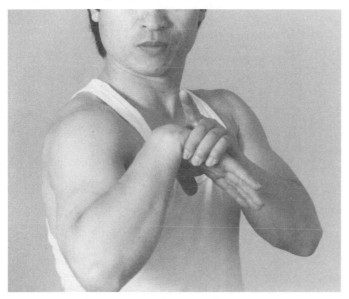

3. Push away from your body.

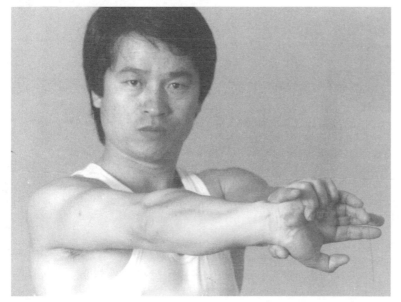

Focus Point: Focus on maintaining your wrist at shoulder height throughout the movement.

Wrist Bend

10-12 Simple, alternate sides

Primary Benefit: Stretches the wrist and the lower forearm.

Martial Arts Application: A good warm-up and conditioning for joint locking, striking and weapon practice.

How to Perform:

1. Stand with your arms in a relaxed ninety-degree bend in front of you, hands out, thumbs pointing to the ceiling.

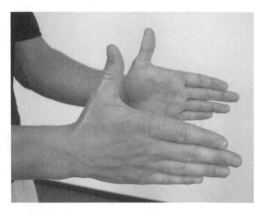

Focus Point: Fix your elbow position at 90° and move your hands and forearms only.

2. Pull your thumbs back toward your chest.

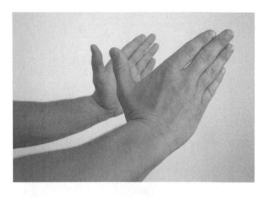

3. Push your little fingers down toward the floor.

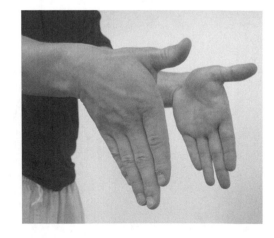

Finger Press

10-12 Simple

Primary Benefit: Stretches the muscles of the fingers, hands and forearms.

Martial Arts Application: Improves strength and flexibility of the grip for grappling, locking, striking and weapon practice.

How to Perform:

1. Stretch your arms in front of you and interlock your fingers with your thumbs facing downward.

2. Stretch and flex your elbows.

Focus Point: Exhale on the outward or downward movement and inhale on the upward or inward movement.

Variations:

Press downward (thumbs facing toward your abdomen) then press upward (thumbs facing away from you).

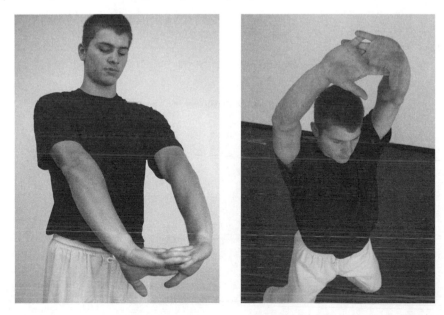

Finger Pull

2-4 Simple, alternate sides

Primary Benefit: Stretches the muscles of the fingers and hands.

Martial Arts Application: Prevents stiffness in the grip.

How to Perform:

1.   Grasp one finger. Keeping your wrist flat, gently pull the finger back toward your forearm.

2.   Perform on each finger and thumb individually.

Focus Point: Focus on pulling gently while trying to minimize the resistance in the finger being stretched.

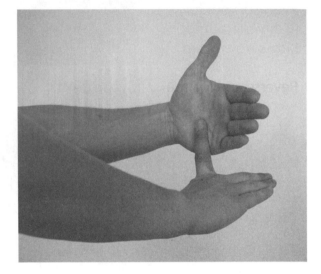

Variation:

To emulate actual combat situations, you can turn your arm over, so your palm is facing upward.

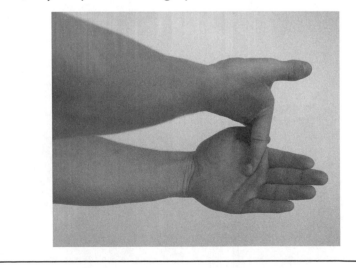

Fist Roll

10-12 Simple

Primary Benefit: Loosens the muscles in the wrist and back of the hand.

Martial Arts Application: Conditioning and warm-up for joint locks, striking and grappling.

How to Perform:

1. Stand with your arms in a relaxed ninety-degree bend in front of you, hands out, thumbs pointing to the ceiling.

2. Make fists with both hands and roll your fists up toward your wrists.

3. Reverse and roll the opposite way.

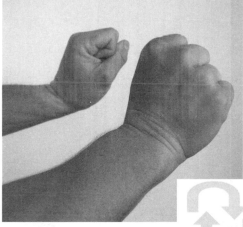

Focus Point: Your index finger knuckle is the anchor point of the rotation.

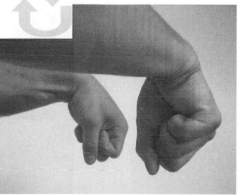

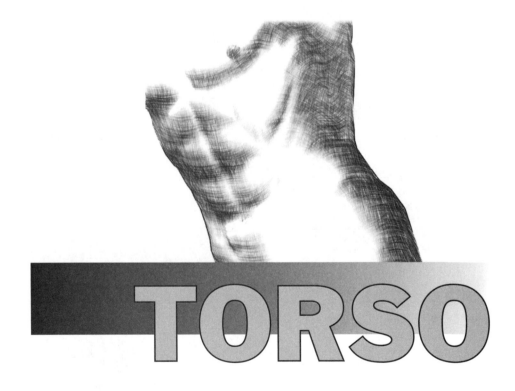

TORSO

Side Bends

8-10 Simple, alternate sides

Primary Benefit: Stretches the oblique muscles.

Martial Arts Application: Improves flexibility for throwing and striking.

How to Perform:

1. Standing, raise your right arm and stretch it over your head.

2. Bend to the left, reaching over your head to toward the floor. Align your arm with your ear as you reach.

Focus Point: Focus on aligning your elbows, head, knees and feet on the same plane. Do not lean forward or backward.

Side Stretch

2-4 Progressive, alternate sides

Primary Benefit: Stretches the large muscles of the torso, lower back, hip and legs.

Martial Arts Application: Improves flexibility for throwing and striking.

How to Perform:

1. Stand with your feet three to four feet apart, your left foot slightly turned in and your right foot at a ninety-degree angle.

2. Extend your arms to the sides at shoulder height and bend to the right, letting your hip shift backwards.

3. Touch the floor beside your right foot and look upwards at your outstretched left hand.

Focus Point: Focus on extending both arms outward away from the chest to open the chest muscles and elongate the torso.

Moving Torso Bend

10-12 Simple

Primary Benefit: Stretches the muscles in the chest, abdominal and spinal areas.

Martial Arts Application: Increases the range of torso movement in throwing and takedowns.

How to Perform:

1. Stand with both feet shoulder width apart and arms outstretched.

2. Bend forward and touch the ground in front of you.

3. Reach through your legs and touch the ground behind you.

4. Stand up and lean back, placing your hands on your hip and opening your chest.

Focus Point:
Support your back when you lean to the rear and relax your spine when leaning forward.

Lunging Side Twist

2-4 Progressive, alternate sides

Primary Benefit: Stretches oblique, groin and hamstring muscles.

Martial Arts Application: Increases range of motion for spinning and twisting movements, such as those in jumping kicks or stick/sword practice.

How to Perform:

1. Stand with your feet about four feet apart, your back foot slightly turned in and your front foot facing forward.

2. Bend your front knee and twist your upper body so your rear arm is tucked against the outside of your front leg.

3. Extend your other arm straight out from your body beside your ear.

Focus Point: Focus on keeping your extended arm, torso and legs on one plane.

Partner Torso Twist   *8-10 Simple, alternate sides*

Primary Benefit: Stretches the large muscles groups of the torso, including the latissimus dorsi (back) and abdominal oblique muscles.

Martial Arts Application: Improves spinning and throwing skills.

How to Perform:

1. Stand back to back with a partner.

2. Both partners twist their upper body to the right and touch palms.

Focus Point: Spot your partner (visually) on each turn to practice orienting yourself in motion.

Variation: One partner twists to the left while the other goes right.

Seated Torso Twist

2-4 Progressive, alternate

Primary Benefit: Stretches the large muscles groups of the torso, including the latissimus dorsi (back) and abdominal oblique muscles.

Martial Arts Application: Improves flexibility for striking, throwing and spinning skills.

How to Perform:

1. Sit with your left leg crossed over your right leg.

2. Put your right arm on your left leg and turn to your left, supporting yourself with your left hand. Look to the rear.

Focus point: Focus on stretching with your breathing—lengthen the spine as you inhale and twist into the stretch as you exhale.

Hybrid Torso Twist

2-4 Progressive, alternate sides

Primary Benefit: Stretches the large muscle groups of the torso, low back, hip and legs including the latissimus dorsi (back), abdominal oblique and quadriceps muscles.

Martial Arts Application: Improves flexibility for grappling, kicking and spinning skills.

How to Perform:

1. Sit with your legs comfortably split.

2. Twist to your right, placing your hands on the floor—your right hand behind your hip and your left hand behind your knee.

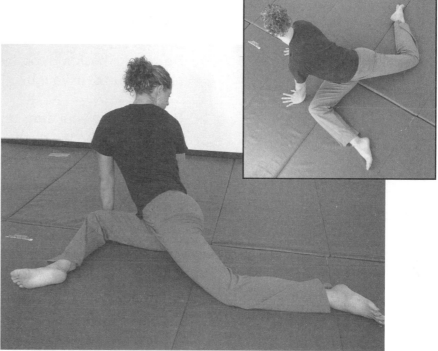

3. As you lower your upper body to the floor, bend your knees and relax your feet.

Focus Point: At the maximum point of the twist, use your rear knee for leverage to increase the stretch in your torso.

Elongation Stretch

3-6 Simple

Primary Benefit: Stretches the large muscles of the torso, arms and legs

Martial Arts Application: Excellent warm-up or cool down stretch for total body relaxation.

How to Perform:

1. Lie on your back with both legs extended and your arms reaching up over your head.

2. Gently stretch your arms up through your fingers. Point your toes and release your pelvis and lower back as you lengthen your legs.

Focus Point: Focus on lengthening the whole body from the spine, elongating all of the major areas of the body: arms, spine and legs.

Full Body Arch

3-6 Simple

Primary Benefit: Improves flexibility across the front of the body, including the abs and quads.

Martial Arts Application: Good warm-up for all movements.

How to Perform:

Lying on your back, point your toes and press your hands into the floor while arching your pelvis up off the floor.

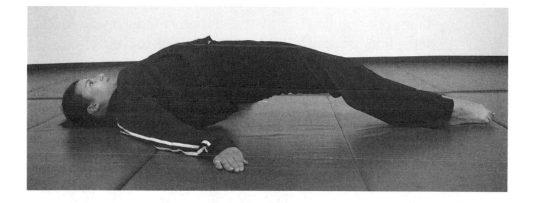

Focus point: Focus on spreading your weight evenly across your heels, shoulder blades and arms. Release tension in the torso.

Lying Torso Twist

2-4 Progressive, alternate

Primary Benefit: Stretches the large muscles groups of the torso, hip and low back, abdominal oblique, hamstrings and quadriceps muscles.

Martial Arts Application: Improves flexibility for grappling, kicking (especially roundhouse kick and crescent kick) and spinning skills.

How to Perform:

1. Lie on your back with both arms outstretched to the side.

2. Raise your right leg and twist your body to touch your foot to the floor on your left side. You may look to the right to increase the stretch.

Focus Point: Focus on keeping both shoulders flat on the floor.

Beginner variation:

1. Lie on your back with both arms outstretched to the side.

2. Raise your right knee and twist your body to touch your knee to the floor on your left side.

Advanced variation:

1. Lie on your stomach.

2. Raise your right leg and touch your right foot to your left hand behind you.

Lunging Side Stretch

2-4 Progressive, alternate

Primary Benefit: Stretches the large muscles of the torso and legs.

Martial Arts Application: Improves strength and flexibility for throwing and falling.

How to Perform:

1. Stand with your feet about four feet apart, your left foot slightly turned in and your right foot at a ninety-degree angle.

2. Extend your arms to the sides at shoulder height and bend to the right, flexing your right knee to a ninety-degree angle and keeping your right thigh parallel to the floor.

3. Rest your right elbow on your thigh and reach your left arm up toward the ceiling, beside your left ear.

Focus point: Focus on keeping your head, hip and feet aligned as you stretch.

Beginner variation:

Easier

1. Stand with your feet about four feet apart, your left foot slightly turned in and your right foot at a ninety-degree angle. Place a chair in front of your hips.

2. Place your hands or forearms on the back of the chair (at chest height) for support and bend to the right, flexing your right knee to a ninety-degree angle and keeping your right thigh parallel to the floor.

Advanced variation:

1. Stand with your feet about four feet apart, your left foot slightly turned in and your right foot at a ninety-degree angle.

Harder

2. Extend your arms to the sides at shoulder height and bend to the right, flexing your right knee to a ninety-degree angle and keeping your right thigh parallel to the floor.

3. Place your right hand on the floor beside your right foot. Focus on keeping your head, hip and feet aligned as you stretch.

Bridge

1-3 Progressive

Primary Benefit: Improves overall torso flexibility.

Martial Arts Application: Strengthens and loosens the torso muscles to improve jumping, kicking and grappling skills.

How to Perform:

1. Lie on your back with your knees bent and feet flat on the floor.

2. Place your palms on the floor next to your head and raise your body up onto your hands and feet.

Focus Point: Create a firm base with your legs so you can relax your upper body.

Easier

Beginner variation 1:

Kneel with your knees together and bend backward, touching your hands to the soles of your feet while looking upward.

Caution: The bridge puts pressure on the spine. If you have back pain or a pre-existing back injury, do not perform this exercise.

Beginner variation 2:
Lie on your back, with your knees bent. Bring your feet in towards your shoulders while raising your buttocks off the floor. Hold your ankles for support while keeping your hip raised as high off the ground as is comfortable.

Beginner variation 3:
Progress to a supported bridge, with a partner supporting your lower back while she helps you push up into the stretch.

Advanced variation:
Lift up onto your toes to intensify the stretch.

BACK

Torso Twist

8-12 Simple, alternate sides

Primary Benefit: Stretches the upper and lower back and the oblique muscles.

Martial Arts Application: Improves agility in falling, grappling, throwing skills and spinning strikes.

How to Perform:

1. Stand with your feet a bit more than shoulder width apart and your arms stretched out to the side.

2. Bend forward at the waist and alternately touch your toes with your outstretched arms.

Focus point: Focus on twisting and bending from the hips.

Spinal Roll at the Bar

8-10 Simple

Primary Benefit: Loosens the spinal column.

Martial Arts Application: Works as a both a warm up and strengthening exercise for the much used large muscles of the back and pelvis.

How to Perform:

1. Bend at the waist and put both hands lightly on the bar for balance.

Focus Point: Focus on a smooth rhythmic movement, like a wave in the ocean.

2. Release your spine by flexing your knees slightly and dropping your abdomen toward the floor while you look upward.

3. Raise up onto your toes, hunching your shoulders and lengthening your spine. Imagine being pulled upward by a string attached to your shoulder blades. Relax your head and neck.

Seated Stick Twist

8-12 Simple

Primary Benefit: Improves flexibility around the spine.

Martial Arts Application: Increases flexibility for striking and weapon techniques.

How to Perform:

1. Sit on a bench or stand in horse riding stance. Plant your feet wide enough to stabilize your hip.

2. Rest a long stick across your shoulders and grasp it with both hands at a comfortable distance from your shoulders.

3. Turn to the right, looking over your right shoulder then to the left looking over your left shoulder

Focus point: Focus on keeping your hip and legs still while getting maximum range of motion above the waist.

Back Stretch

2-4 Progressive

Primary Benefit: Stretches the back and shoulders.

Martial Arts Application: Relaxes the back muscles in preparation for all types of practice.

How to Perform:

1. Kneel on your hands and knees.

2. Sink your buttocks backward onto your feet, point your toes under you.

3. Slide your hands forward along the floor to increase the stretch.

Focus Point: Focus on pressing your low back straight down into the floor.

Cat Stretch

8-10 Simple

Primary Benefit: Stretches and strengthens the back.

Martial Arts Application: A good warm up for all types of practice.

How to Perform:

1. Kneel on your hands and knees. Look at the floor but do not drop your head.

2. Inhale while curling your spine up toward the ceiling.

3. Exhale while pressing your spine down toward the floor.

Focus Point: Keep your head and pelvis level while trying for maximum movement in the spine.

Back Roll

8-12 Simple

Primary Benefit: Stretches the back.

Martial Arts Application: Strengthens and loosens the spine for falling and throwing.

How to Perform:

1. Sit with your knees bent and your hands clasped around your thighs or shins.

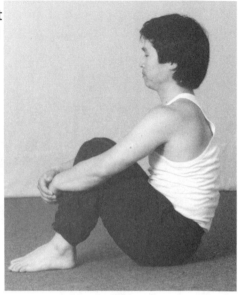

2. Gently roll back until your shoulder blades touch the floor and then roll up to the starting position. If you have difficulty rolling back up, try stretching your arms toward your feet, rather than grasping your legs.

Focus Point: Focus on rounding your back by keeping your chin tucked to your chest.

Back Curl   *6-10 Simple*

Primary Benefit: Stretches the back.

Martial Arts Application: Strengthens and loosens the spine for falling and throwing.

How to Perform:

1. Lie on your back with your knees bent.

2. Pull your knees to your chest and while lifting your head to meet your knees.

Focus Point: Focus on lifting your shoulders and flattening your lower back on the floor.

Back Bend at the Bar

1-3 Progressive, alternate

Primary Benefit: Loosens the spinal column and stretches the large muscles of the legs.

Martial Arts Application: Increases kicking height and range and acrobatic kicks.

How to Perform:

1. Stand about one foot from the bar, with your hands resting on the bar, and allow your partner to lift your leg to about waist height.

2. Slowly bend your upper body backward toward the bar while letting your hands slide outward along the bar.

Focus Point: Focus on aligning your body from your straightened spine downward.

Caution: Do not perform this exercise, if you have a preexisting back injury or experience back pain during the exercise.

3. If you are very flexible, once you have reached an upper body arch, raise up onto your toes while your partner maintains the height of your outstretched leg.

Seated Reaches

3-6 Simple, alternate sides

Primary Benefit: Stretches the muscles along the sides of the torso.

Martial Arts Application: Improves flexibility for twisting and spinning movements, as well as defensive body movements (i.e. bobbing and weaving).

How to Perform:

1. Sit with your legs split to a comfortable angle and your arms outstretched at shoulder height.

Focus Point:
Focus on keeping your spine and your head erect.

2. While looking straight ahead, reach your right hand as far as you can to the right without bending your spine.

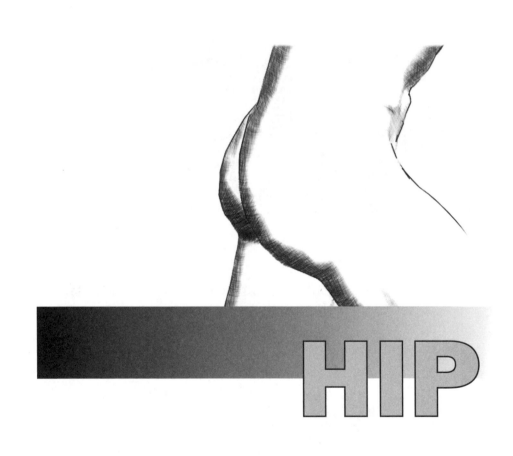

HIP

Hip Rotation

8-10 Simple

Primary Benefit: Improves flexibility in the hip joint.

Martial Arts Application: Prepares the body for activity of all kinds.

How to Perform:

1. Place your hands on your waist and rotate your hip clockwise.

2. Reverse and rotate counterclockwise.

*Focus Point: Roll your pelvis in a
smooth gliding motion.*

Slump

6-8 Simple, alternate sides

Primary Benefit: Stretches the groin and hamstrings.

Martial Arts Application: Improves flexibility for grappling and kicking.

How to Perform:

1. Stand with one foot on a chair and the other on the floor beside the chair.

2. Bend straight forward at the waist, letting your upper body relax toward the floor.

Focus Point: Focus on keeping your torso bent at a ninety degree angle, with your thigh perpendicular to your torso and your hip square to the front.

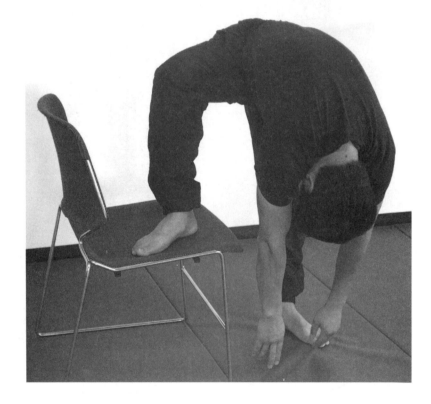

Cross Legged Side Bend

8-10 Simple, alternate sides

Primary Benefit: Improves flexibility in the obliques, lower back, buttocks, hamstrings and calves.

Martial Arts Application: Prepares the body for throwing, grappling, weapons and striking techniques.

How to Perform:

1. Stand with your feet together, crossed at the ankles.

2. Bend to the right side, reaching for your left ankle. Keep both feet flat on the ground and both knees straight.

Focus point: Focus on relaxing the hamstrings and hip. Bending the lower back is a secondary goal.

Standing Piriformis Stretch *2-4 Progressive, alternate*

Primary Benefit: Stretches the muscles of the buttocks and hip.

Martial Arts Application: Prepares the buttocks muscles for kicking.

How to Perform:

1. Stand facing a low (hip high) stretching bar.

2. Place your lower leg and foot along the top of the stretching bar.

3. Lean forward into the stretch.

Focus Point: Focus on keeping the side of your lower leg flat along the bar so you feel the stretch deep within your buttocks.

Modified Squats at the Bar

2-4 Progressive, alternate sides

Primary Benefit: Improves flexibility in the buttocks and abductor muscles.

Martial Arts Application: Increases flexibility for kicking, stances and grappling skills.

How to Perform:

1. Facing the bar, bend at the waist and place your hands on the bar for support.

Focus Point: Decrease the amount of weight place on your standing leg to increase the stretch in your other leg.

2. Flex your left knee and lower your body, bringing your right knee under your left leg. Keep your right foot pointed.

Caution: Do not perform this exercise if you have a preexisting knee injury or experience knee pain during the exercise.

Partner Groin Stretch

2-4 Progressive, alternate

Primary Benefit: Stretches the muscles of the groin and hip.

Martial Arts Application: Improves kicking height and range, especially for side, back and spinning kicks.

How to Perform:

1. Stand facing a wall or stretching bar, with your partner standing beside you.

2. Place your hands on the wall, lean slightly forward and lift your leg to the side like you are chambering a roundhouse kick.

3. When you are ready, your partner raises your leg to the side, keeping your thigh and calf parallel to the ground and your knee at a ninety-degree angle.

Focus Point: Focus on keeping your hip square to your partner and your spine straight.

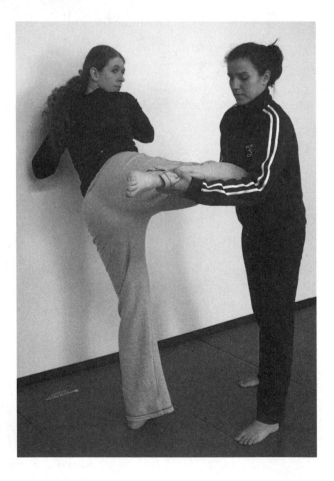

Squat

2-4 Progressive

Primary Benefit: Stretches the hip, groin and lower back muscles, as well as the heels and ankles.

Martial Arts Application: Improves range of motion in the legs and lower back for kicking, throwing and grappling.

How to Perform:

1. Stand with your feet slightly more than shoulder width apart.

2. Slowly lower your buttocks, toward the floor, dropping your weight between your feet.

3. To balance in the squat position, lean your upper body slightly forward and place your hands between your feet.

4. To increase the stretch, use your elbows to push outward on your knees.

Focus point: Focus on distributing your weight equally over both feet and sinking your hip into the squat.

Caution: Stop if you experience knee pain at any time during the stretch. Squatting is not recommended if you have had knee pain or a knee injury in the past.

Butterfly Stretch

2-4 Progressive

Primary Benefit: Stretches the hip, groin and thigh muscles.

Martial Arts Application: Improves kicking range.

How to Perform:

1. Sit with your knees bent and the soles of your feet touching.

2. Straighten your spine by sitting against a wall or putting your hands behind you, palms flat on the floor for support.

3. To deepen the stretch, move your feet closer to your thighs.

Focus point: Focus on stretching equally across the inner thighs. You may feel the stretch more in one leg than the other at first, but do not push the more flexible leg until the less flexible one "catches up."

Caution: Do not allow anyone to stand on or put their full body weight on your legs during this exercise.

Advanced Butterfly Stretch   *2-4 Progressive*

Primary Benefit: Stretches the lower back, hip, groin and thigh muscles.

Martial Arts Application: Improves kicking range.

How to Perform:

1. Sit with your knees bent and the soles of your feet touching.

2. Lean forward from the waist, setting your elbows on the floor in front of you or applying pressure to your knees with your arms.

Focus point: Focus on bending from the lower back and hip while keeping your spine straight.

Caution: Do not allow anyone to stand on or put their full body weight on your legs during this exercise.

Knee Pull

2-4 Progressive, alternate sides

Primary Benefit: Stretches the lower back, buttocks, groin and hamstring muscles.

Martial Arts Application: Improves kicking range in advanced kicks such as twisting kicks and crescent kicks.

How to Perform:

1. Seated, bend your knee and pull it toward your chest with both arms.

2. A number of methods can be used to pull your leg: place both hands on your ankle (over the top or cradling your leg) or place one hand on your ankle and one on your knee. If you have had knee pain in the past, the second method is safest.

Focus Point: Focus on pulling the leg as one unit to avoid stressing the knee. You should feel a slight twist in the deep muscles at the top of your leg and in your buttocks.

If you experience knee pain, try this variation.

Single Leg Pull

2-4 Progressive, alternate sides

Primary Benefit: Stretches the hamstrings and hip muscles.

Martial Arts Application: Improves flexibility for kicking.

How to Perform:

1. Lie on your back with both legs extended.

2. Grasp one foot and extend the leg out to the side, bringing it to rest on the floor beside you. Open your pelvis and keep your back as flat on the floor as possible.

Focus Point: Focus on opening your pelvis and keeping your spine flat on the floor.

Prone Hip Rotation

10-12 Simple, alternate sides

Primary Benefit: Improves flexibility in the pelvis.

Martial Arts Application: Good warm-up for footwork, kicking or ground work.

How to Perform:

1. Lie on your back with your knees bent and your back flat to the floor.

2. Raise one knee and draw a circle in the air with it. You may use your hand to support your knee if necessary.

Focus Point: Firmly plant your supporting leg to isolate the movement in your other leg.

Frog Stretch

2-4 Progressive

Primary Benefit: Stretches the adductor muscles in the inside of the upper thighs.

Martial Arts Application: Improves flexibility for kicking and grappling.

How to Perform:

1. Kneel with your feet turned outward and your elbows on the floor.

2. Slowly spread your knees outward as you slide your hands forward on the floor.

Focus Point: Press your hip down toward the floor to deepen the stretch.

3. If you can do so comfortably, let your pelvis and chest come to rest on the floor.

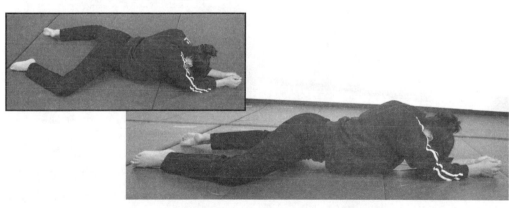

Y Stretch

2-4 Progressive, alternate sides

Primary Benefit: Stretches the muscles in the torso, hip and thighs.

Martial Arts Application: Improves flexibility for spinning, twisting and turning movements as well as ground work.

How to Perform:

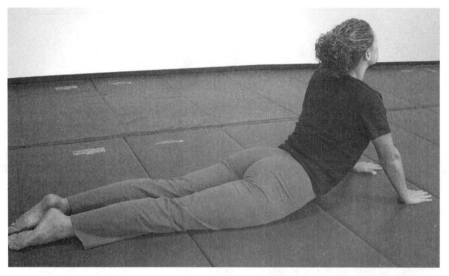

1. Begin on your stomach with your chest raised and arms extended.

2. Swing your right leg over your left, stretching as far to the right as possible, while looking to the front.

Focus Point: Focus on swinging the leg in a smooth motion while keeping the stationary leg anchored to the floor.

Cross Knee Pull

6-8 Simple, alternate sides

Primary Benefit: Stretches the lower back, buttocks and outside upper thighs.

Martial Arts Application: Improves kicking range.

How to Perform:

1. Lie on your back with your left foot flat on the floor and your right ankle resting just above your left knee.

Focus Point: Focus on relaxing your stretching leg and not resisting the pull.

2. With both hands, pull your left leg toward you until you feel a stretch in your right thigh.

Partner Piriformis Stretch   *2-4 Progressive, alternate*

Primary Benefit: Stretches the muscles of the buttocks and hip.

Martial Arts Application: Prepares the buttocks muscles for kicking.

How to Perform:

1. Lie on your back and raise one leg with your knee bent.

2. Your partner steadies your knee with one hand while grasping your ankle with the other.

Focus Point: Focus on keeping your lower leg perpendicular to your torso throughout the stretch.

3. When you are ready, your partner gently pulls your knee toward him (to maintain the angle of the stretch) while pushing your leg toward you.

Bridge and Roll

8-10 Simple, alternate

Primary Benefit: Stretches the muscles of the torso and hip.

Martial Arts Application: Prepares the body for groundwork and grappling.

How to Perform:

1. Lie on your back with your feet flat on the floor, knees bent and arms up in a "ready" position. Bridge up onto your shoulders. Tuck your chin.

Focus Point: Focus on thrusting your pelvis upward as you turn.

2. Roll to the right, onto your right shoulder. Look and reach to the right.

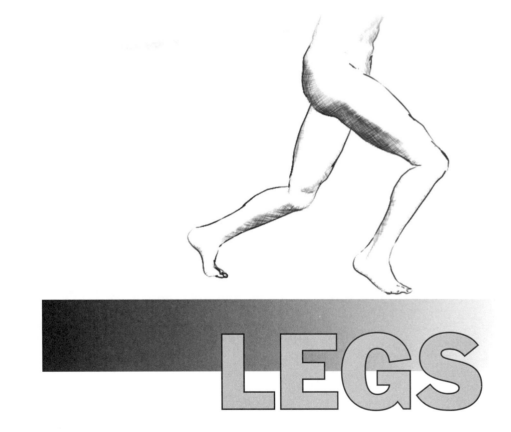

LEGS

Knee Rotation

10-12 Simple

Primary Benefit: Improves flexibility in the knees.

Martial Arts Application: Good warm-up for footwork, kicking or ground work.

How to Perform:

1. Stand with both knees together.

2. Place your hands on your knees and rotate them clockwise.

3. Reverse and rotate counter clockwise.

Focus Point: Stabilize your head position above your feet.

Knee Raises

8-12 Simple, alternate sides

Primary Benefit: Improves flexibility in the hip joint and hamstrings while strengthening the legs.

Martial Arts Application: Increases kicking height, range, speed and power.

Focus Point: Relax your feet and focus on lifting from your knees.

How to Perform:

1. Stand with your feet shoulder width apart.

2. Raise one knee up as high as you can. Relax your upper body, letting your arms rotate close to your torso.

Beginner variation:

Lean your back against a wall and have a partner push your knee up to your chest and hold it.

Advanced variation 1:

Twist to touch your knee to the opposite elbow.

Advanced variation 2:

Rotate the leg outward ninety degrees to open the hip.

Abductor Stretch

2-4 Progressive, alternate sides

Primary Benefit: Stretches the muscles of the outer legs and hip.

Martial Arts Application: Increases kicking height and range, particularly for side kick and spinning kicks (hip turning agility).

How to Perform:

1. Stand sideways next to a wall.

2. Place your left arm on the wall, with your palm flat on the wall and fingers pointing toward the ceiling.

3. Leaning your left hip into the wall, cross your left leg behind your right leg.

Focus Point: Focus on slowly pushing your hip toward the wall while keeping your upper body erect.

Calf Stretch

2-4 Progressive, alternate sides

Primary Benefit: Increases flexibility in the back of the lower leg.

Martial Arts Application: Improves jumping, kicking, footwork and low stances.

How to Perform:

1. Stand about arms' length from a wall and place your palms on the wall at shoulder height.

2. Step back with your right foot, bending your left knee, while keeping your right leg straight and your right heel on the floor.

Focus Point: Focus on keeping your heel flat on the floor and your foot pointed at the wall. If your heel leaves the floor, you are no longer isolating your calf muscles.

Toe Touch

2-4 Progressive

Primary Benefit: Improves flexibility in the lower back, buttocks, hamstrings and calves.

Martial Arts Application: Improves kicking height and stance depth.

How to Perform:

Focus point: Focus on relaxing the hamstrings. Touching the floor is a secondary goal.

1. Stand with both feet together and knees straight.

2. Bend at the waist and touch your toes with your hands.

Beginner variation 1:

Begin in a squat with both palms on the floor then stand up as far as you can while maintaining your hand position.

Beginner variation 2:

If the conventional toe touch is too difficult, use a chair or stretching bar for support, bending forward at the hips and resting your hands on the back of the chair or the bar.

Advanced variation 1:

Touch your palms to the floor.

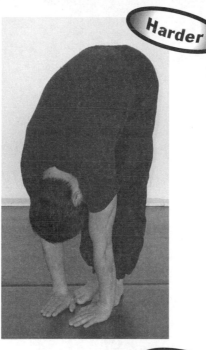

Advanced variation 2:

Cross your legs and touch your toes.

Caution: If you feel dizzy, stand up slowly. If you often feel dizzy during the toe touch, try Beginner variation 2, keeping your head above waist level. If you have knee pain during this stretch, try Beginner variation 2 and do not lock your knees out.

Twisting Toe Touch

2-4 Progressive, alternate

Primary Benefit: Improves flexibility in the lower back, buttocks, hamstrings and calves.

Martial Arts Application: Improves kicking height and stance depth.

How to Perform:

1. Standing with both feet together, flex your knees and twist your upper body to the side, reaching down to touch the floor on your right side with both hands.

Focus point: Try to keep your feet and knees facing forward throughout the exercise.

2. Slowly stand up as far as you can, keeping your hands on the floor.

Windmills

8-10 Simple, alternate sides

Primary Benefit: Improves flexibility in the lower back, buttocks, hamstrings and calves.

Martial Arts Application: Improves kicking height, particularly for twisting or spinning kicks.

How to Perform:

1. Cross your feet and stretch your arms out to the sides.

2. Keeping your legs straight, reach your right hand to the outside of your left ankle. Reach your left hand toward the sky and look at your fingertips.

Focus point: Bend from the hip to maintain the structure of your spine and shoulders as you reach toward your ankle.

Lunging Forward Stretch *2-4 Progressive, alternate*

Primary Benefit: Stretches the hip and leg muscles.

Martial Arts Application: Improves flexibility for deep stances and kicking.

How to Perform:

1. Stand with your feet about four feet apart, your left foot slightly turned in and your right foot at a ninety-degree angle.

2. Extend your arms above your head and lunge forward, flexing your right knee to a ninety-degree angle and keeping your right thigh parallel to the floor.

Focus point: Focus on keeping your pelvis square to the front and your spine straight and erect.

Single Leg Stretch   *2-4 Progressive, alternate sides*

Primary Benefit: Stretches the hip and quadriceps muscles.

Martial Arts Application: Increases kicking height and range as well as balance.

How to Perform:

1. Stand on your right leg and raise your left leg behind you.

2. Grasp your left ankle with your left hand and pull it up and toward you while lowering your upper body. Make sure you are pulling on your ankle, not your foot during this stretch.

Focus Point: Focus on slow moving balance as you stretch.

Standing Quad Stretch

2-4 Progressive, alternate

Primary Benefit: Stretches the front of the thigh.

Martial Arts Application: Increases kicking height and range and improves range of motion for leg blocks.

How to Perform:

1. Stand on your left leg and bend your right leg until you can grasp your right ankle behind you.

2. Let your right foot relax as you stretch. Do not pull on your foot.

Focus Point: Focus on keeping your calf and thigh aligned under your hip so your leg does not rotate outward.

Toe Raises at the Bar

8-10 Simple

Primary Benefit: Loosens the muscles of the pelvis and the backs of the legs.

Martial Arts Application: Improves strength and flexibility for kicking and stances.

How to Perform:

1. Bend at the waist and place both hands lightly on the bar for balance.

2. Flex your knees, keeping your feet flat on the floor.

3. Raise your heels from the floor, maintaining the angle of flexion in your knees.

Focus Point: Maintain a straight spine and focus on the movement in your pelvis and knees.

4. Straighten your knees while staying up on your toes.

Individual Leg Raises

2-4 Progressive, alternate

Primary Benefit: Stretches the major muscle groups in the legs and groin.

Martial Arts Application: Increases kicking range and balance.

How to Perform:

1. Standing, place your leg on a stretching bar or other firm support at about waist height. Your standing foot should be parallel to the stretching bar.

2. Loop a belt around your foot and pull back slowly, maintaining an upright posture.

Focus Point: Straighten your torso and standing leg and focus on relaxing your upper body.

Leg Extension at the Bar

8-10 Simple, alternate sides

Primary Benefit: Stretches the quadriceps and groin muscles.

Martial Arts Application: Increases kicking height and range, particularly for kicks to the rear or spinning kicks.

How to Perform:

1. Stand facing the bar, with both hands on the bar for support.

2. Relax your head and neck. With your left leg straight, bring your right knee up toward the bar.

Focus Point: Be flexible in the movement of your supporting leg and upper body to create a smooth flowing stretch.

3. Flex your left knee slightly while dropping your upper body down and extending your right leg straight out behind you. Point your toes and try to make your body into the shape of a gentle curve.

4. Bend your right leg, pulling your foot toward your buttocks.

Groin Stretch at the Bar

8-10 Simple, alternate

Primary Benefit: Stretches large muscle groups of the lower back, hip and legs.

Martial Arts Application: Increases kicking height and range, especially axe kick, roundhouse kick and front kick.

How to Perform:

1. Stand at the bar with the toes of your right foot resting on the bar and your hands grasping the bar on either side of your foot for balance.

2. Bend your right knee, deepening the stretch in your hamstrings and calf.

3. If you are very flexible, raise up onto the toes of your left foot, bringing your right knee into your chest.

Focus point: Do not allow either knee to roll outward during this exercise. Keep both knees facing forward at all times.

Stretching Bar Split

2-4 Progressive, alternate sides

Primary Benefit: Stretches the muscles of the groin and legs.

Martial Arts Application: Improves kicking height and range, especially axe kick, crescent kick and high jumping kicks.

How to Perform:

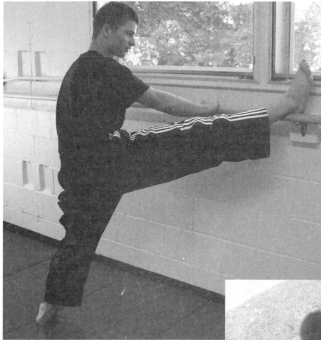

1. Stand facing the stretching bar and place your right ankle on the bar.

2. Slide your ankle to the right, down the bar, to lengthen the stretch. Keep your left foot flat on the ground.

Focus Point: Focus on keeping your hip square to the wall and your spine erect.

Partner Front Leg Raise *2-4 Progressive, alternate*

Primary Benefit: Stretches the major muscle groups in the legs and groin.

Martial Arts Application: Increases height and range for front, axe, crescent and raising kicks.

How to Perform:

1. Standing, place one leg on your partner's shoulder or have your partner raise one leg up in front of you without bending your knee.

2. When you are ready, your partner moves lower by sliding his back leg backward into a low stance, deepening the stretch.

Caution: Indicate to your partner when to stop and hold the stretch to prevent overstretching.

Beginner variation:

If you cannot place your leg on your partner's shoulder or your partner is not strong enough to confidently support you, use a wall or stretching bar for support while your partner raises your leg.

Focus Point: Focus on keeping your hip square to the front and your upper body as erect as possible.

Partner Side Leg Raise

2-4 Progressive, alternate

Primary Benefit: Stretches the major muscle groups in the legs and groin.

Martial Arts Application: Increases height and range for side, hook and whip kicks.

How to Perform:

1. Standing, place one leg on your partner's shoulder or have your partner raise one leg to the side of you without bending your knee. Clasp hands with your partner for balance, if necessary.

2. When you are ready, your partner deepens the stretch by sliding his back leg backward into a low stance.

Caution: Indicate to your partner when to stop and hold the stretch to prevent overstretching.

Beginner variation:

If you cannot place your leg on your partner's shoulder or your partner is not strong enough to confidently support you, use a wall or stretching bar for support while your partner raises your leg.

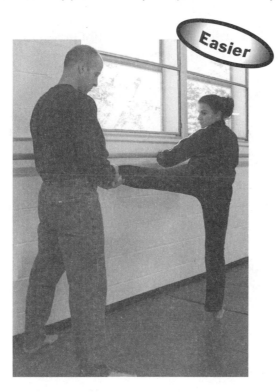

Focus Point: Focus on keeping your head, hip, knee and feet aligned, and your upper body as erect as possible.

Partner Rear Leg Raise

2-4 Progressive, alternate

Primary Benefit: Stretches the major muscle groups in the legs and groin.

Martial Arts Application: Increases height and range for back kick, front kick, raising kicks and spinning kicks.

How to Perform:

1. Facing away from your partner, lean forward. Steady yourself with your hands on the ground or on your knee.

2. Reach up and backward with your leg to place it on your partner's shoulder as she stands in a low front stance or have your partner raise your leg.

3. When you are ready, your partner stands upward, increasing the stretch as you maintain your balance,.

Focus Point: Focus on keeping your head, hip, knee and feet aligned.

Caution: Indicate to your partner when to stop and hold the stretch to prevent overstretching.

Beginner variation:

If you cannot place your leg on your partner's shoulder or your partner is not strong enough to confidently support you, use a wall or stretching bar for support while your partner raises your leg.

Controlled Kicks

6-10 Simple, alternate sides

Primary Benefit: Improves flexibility and strength in the legs.

Martial Arts Application: Increases kicking height, range and control.

Focus Point: Focus on controlling the progression of the movement (angle of chambering, weight transfer, pivot, range of motion and retraction) at your optimum height. Raw kicking height is a secondary goal.

How to Perform for Front Kick, Raising Kick or any Linear Kick:

1. Stand in a left foot forward fighting stance, with your right hand resting lightly on the bar beside you (the bar is on your right side).

2. Raise your right knee and slowly extend into a front kick, using the bar as a light support. Kick as high as you are able to without support.

3. Hold for a count of 3 to 10, depending on your ability level. Retract your leg slowly and return to fighting stance.

How to Perform for Side Kick or Roundhouse Kick:

1. Stand in a right foot forward fighting stance with your right hand resting lightly on the bar (the bar is on your right side).

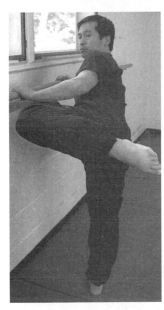

2. Raise your left knee, turn and slowly extend into a side kick, placing both hands on the bar for light support. Kick as high as you are able without support.

3. Hold for a count of 3 to 10, depending on your ability level. Retract the leg slowly and return to fighting stance.

How to Perform for Spinning Kicks:

1. Stand in a right foot forward fighting stance (the bar is on your right side).

2. Turn counterclockwise toward the bar, raise your left knee, and slowly extend into the kick, placing both hands on the bar for light support. Kick as high as you are able without support.

3. Hold for a count of 3 to 10, depending on your ability level. Retract the leg slowly and return to fighting stance.

Partner Controlled Kicks   *6-10 Simple, alternate sides*

Primary Benefit: Improves flexibility and strength in the legs

Martial Arts Application: Increases strength, flexibility and control in kicks.

How to Perform:

1. At the stretching bar, choose a kick from the Controlled Kicks exercise on the previous pages and perform steps 1 and 2 of the exercise.

2. When your kick reaches its maximum extension, have your partner lightly grasp your shin (or your lower thigh if you experience knee pain) and raise your leg another 1-3 inches.

Focus Point: To increase the length of time you can hold each kick, focus on the equilibrium between your upper and lower body. The primary goal, however, is to maintain a perfect kick for a short duration rather an imperfect movement for a longer duration.

3. When your partner removes his supporting hand, try to hold this new height. If necessary, your partner can provide a very light support so that you are doing at least 80% of the work to hold the kick in the air.

Forward Leg Swings

8-12 Simple, alternate sides

Primary Benefit: Improves dynamic flexibility in the legs.

Martial Arts Application: Increases kicking height and range, especially for axe kick and front kick.

How to Perform:

1. Stand in fighting stance at the bar and place your right hand on the bar for light support.

2. Swing your right leg up, loosely and without power, focusing on a dynamic initiation of the swing.

3. Let it fall and swing past your left foot.

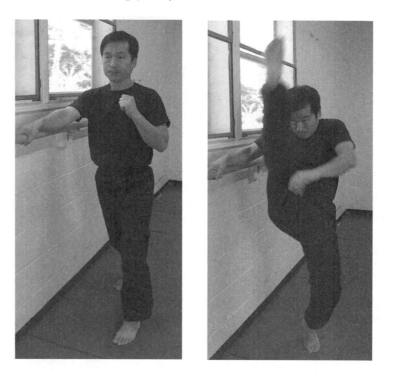

Focus Point: Begin with smaller swings to relax your leg initially, then progress to larger swings as your muscles warm up.

Lateral Leg Swings

8-12 Simple, alternate sides

Primary Benefit: Improves dynamic flexibility in the legs.

Martial Arts Application: Increases kicking height and range, especially for side kick, hook kick and back kick.

How to Perform:

1. Stand facing the bar and place both hands on the bar for light support.

2. Swing your right leg up to the right, loosely and without power, focusing on a dynamic initiation of the swing.

3. Let it fall and swing past your left foot.

Focus Point: Begin with smaller swings to relax your leg initially, then progress to larger swings as your muscles warm up.

Rear Leg Swings

8-12 Simple, alternate sides

Primary Benefit: Improves dynamic flexibility in the legs.

Martial Arts Application: Increases kicking height and range, especially for back kick, whip kick and spinning kicks.

How to Perform:

1. Stand facing the bar and place both hands on the bar for light support.

2. Swing your right leg up to the rear, loosely and without power, focusing on a dynamic initiation of the swing. Look back over your shoulder at your foot.

3. Let your leg fall and swing slightly through to the front, without touching the wall.

Focus Point: Don't open your hip to the rear when you raise your leg. Focus on keeping your pelvis as square to the wall as possible.

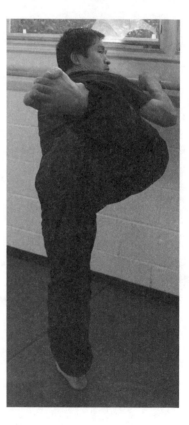

Measured Kicks

Primary Benefit: Improves dynamic flexibility in the legs.

Martial Arts Application: Increases kicking height, range and accuracy.

How to Perform:

1. On a heavy bag, mark 3 to 4 zones, about three inches in height, with the lowest zone at a very comfortable height for your kick.

2. Throw two full power kicks to the lowest zone, two 80% power kicks to the next highest zone and two 50% power kicks to the remaining zones.

3. Finish up by throwing one kick to each of the zones, from lowest to highest.

4. Rest briefly between each kick and focus on accuracy of height.

Focus Point: Pay careful attention to the placement of your support leg so the distance for each kicking height is correct before you begin to kick. This will increase your sensitivity to distance and therefore increase the accuracy of your high kicks.

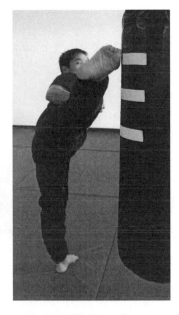

Variations:

Finish (step 3) by kicking middle-low-high or high-middle-low.

Groin Stretch

2-4 Progressive, alternate sides

Primary Benefit: Stretches the groin, hamstring and calf muscles.

Martial Arts Application: Increases kicking height and range, especially for crescent kicks, axe kick and linear kicks.

How to Perform:

1. Stand with your feet about twice your shoulder width apart.

2. Squat to the left side with your left leg bent and your right leg extended. Reach toward your right foot, maintaining an erect spine. Your pelvis should be square to the front.

Focus Point: Incline your upper body slightly forward at the hip while keeping your spine erect.

Standing Split

2-4 Progressive, alternate sides

Primary Benefit: Stretches the groin, hamstrings and quads.

Martial Arts Application: Improves linear kicking height.

How to Perform:

1. Stand a few feet from a wall.

2. Bend forward and place your palms on the floor.

3. Raise one leg behind you with your toes pointed toward the ceiling and slide your foot as far as possible up the wall.

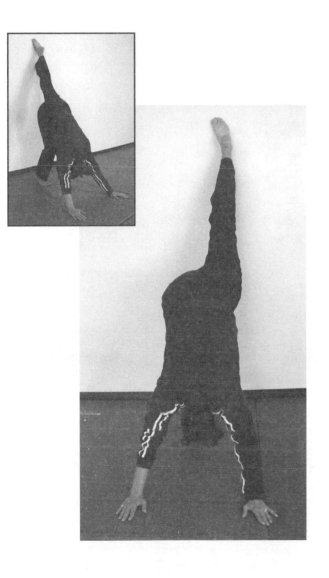

Focus point: Focus on keeping your pelvis square to the floor.

Cross Under

2-4 Progressive, alternate sides

Primary Benefit: Stretches the muscles of the hip, buttocks and outside of the legs as well as the side of the torso.

Martial Arts Application: Improves flexibility for kicking and ground work.

How to Perform:

1. Sit in front of a bench (or heavy bag) with your arms resting on the object for support and most of our weight on your right hip.

2. Cross your left leg over your right, bending it at the knee.

3. Lift your weight onto your left foot, supporting your upper body with your arms, while you stretch your right foot along the floor away from you.

Focus Point: Focus on keeping your upper body as erect as possible.

Kneeling Quad Stretch

2-4 Progressive, alternate sides

Primary Benefit: Stretches the front of the hip and groin muscles.

Martial Arts Application: Improves flexibility for kicking and deep stances.

How to Perform:

1. Kneel on your right knee, placing your left foot on the floor.

2. Slide your right leg backward, allowing your hip to open. Never allow your left knee to extend in front of your left ankle.

Focus point: Focus on pressing your rear thigh toward the floor.

Advanced variation:

Lift the foot of your rear leg toward your spine while you lower your hip downward.

Harder

Caution: If you experience knee pain or have a pre-existing injury to your kneecap or knee cartilage, do not lift your rear foot off the ground

Static Torso Bend

2-4 Progressive

Primary Benefit: Stretches the muscles in the back, hamstrings and calves.

Martial Arts Application: Increases the range of torso movement in throwing, takedowns and falls.

How to Perform:

1. Kneel on all fours with your hands shoulder with apart.

2. Lift your hip and straighten your knees, going up on your toes.

3. If you are comfortable lowering your heels to the floor, do so, letting your head drop slightly for a deeper stretch in your arms and back.

Focus Point: Focus on pressing your chest toward your thighs.

Easier

Beginner variation 1: If you have pain in your hamstrings, flex your knees slightly and keep your heels raised.

Easier

Beginner variation 2: If you have pain in your shoulders, rest your hands on a slightly elevated surface, like a low step.

Double Quadriceps Stretch

2-4 Progressive

Primary Benefit: Stretches the quadriceps muscles, knees and ankles.

Martial Arts Application: Improves kicking initiation speed, flexibility and range of movement on the ground.

How to Perform:

1. Kneel with your toes pointed under your hips. Never turn your feet out during this stretch.

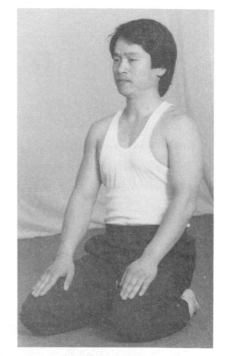

Focus Point: Use your hands and elbows as support to control the depth of the stretch.

2. Lie back with your legs folded under you. If you cannot lie flat, rest your elbows on the floor to ease the stretch to a comfortable position.

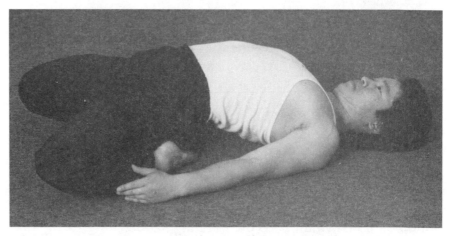

Caution: Stop if you experience knee pain.

Kneeling Groin Stretch

2-4 Progressive, alternate sides

Primary Benefit: Stretches the muscles of the inside upper thigh.

Martial Arts Application: Improves flexibility for kicking, stances and ground work.

How to Perform:

1. Place your left foot flat on the floor and bend your knee so that your shin is perpendicular to the floor. Place your hands on either side of your foot for support and balance.

2. Place your right knee and foot on the floor behind you and slightly out to the right.

3. Lean forward with your upper body and press your pelvis toward the ground. Do not allow your right knee to come forward of your right ankle—maintain the perpendicular angle.

Focus Point: Focus on pressing your hips toward the ground while maintaining the starting position of both feet.

Caution: Stop if you experience knee pain.

Seated Toe Touch

2-4 Progressive

Primary Benefit: Stretches the hamstrings.

Martial Arts Application: Improves kicking height, especially front kick and jumping kicks.

How to Perform:

1. Sit with your legs extended in front of you and together, with your knees straight.

2. Extend your arms in front of you and bend at the waist to touch your hands to your toes.

Focus point: Focus on pressing your thighs down into the floor and pulling your toes back.

Caution: During the partner stretch, the partner leaning forward should indicate if the stretch becomes too painful.

Beginner variation:

1. Sit with your legs extended in front of you and together, with your knees straight.

2. Place your hands behind you, palms flat on the floor. Focus on pressing your thighs down into the ground and pulling your toes backward until you feel a slight stretch.

Advanced variation:

1. Facing a partner, sit in the starting position with the soles of your feet touching.

2. Grasp hands.

3. One partner leans back while the other partner leans forward.

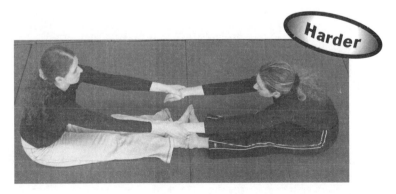

Seated V Stretch

2-4 Progressive, alternate sides

Primary Benefit: Stretches the hamstring, groin and oblique muscles.

Martial Arts Application: Improves kicking height and range, especially side kick, back kick, axe kick and crescent kicks.

How to Perform:

1. Sit with your legs spread as far to sides as you find comfortable.

2. Reach your left arm toward your right thigh while you lean to the left from the hips Reach your right arm over your head toward your left foot.

Focus Point: Focus on bending sideways from your hip. Do not slouch your back or lean forward.

Box Stretch

2-4 Progressive, alternate sides

Primary Benefit: Stretches the hamstrings and low back.

Martial Arts Application: Improves flexibility for techniques on the ground.

How to Perform:

1. Sit facing your partner, with one of your legs bent in front of you and the other outstretched. Your partner's outstretched foot is pressed lightly against your bent leg and your outstretched foot is pressed lightly against your partner's bent leg.

2. Grasp hands or wrists with your partner.

3. Lean backward as your partner bends forward at the waist. Lean only as far as is comfortable for your partner.

4. Repeat the process with your partner leaning back and you bending forward. The forward bending partner should always control the degree of stretch.

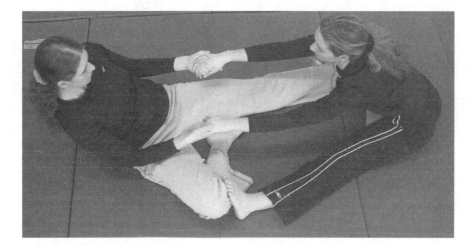

Focus Point: Maintain a straight spine while bending from the waist.

Straddle Stretch

2-4 Progressive

Primary Benefit: Stretches the legs and hip.

Martial Arts Application: Improves kicking height and range.

How to Perform:

1. Seated, spread your legs to the sides.
2. Bend at the waist and stretch forward. Try to keep your toes pointed to the ceiling and your thighs flat on the floor.

Focus Point: Relax your hip joints and shoulders, bringing your focus to pressing your legs into the floor.

3. Stretch to the right foot.
4. Stretch to the left foot.

Beginner variation:

If you cannot reach your foot, loop a belt around the arch of your foot and gently pull toward you.

Advanced variation:

1. Sit facing a partner in the starting position with your feet touching.

2. Grasp hands.

3. One partner lies back while the other leans forward.

Hurdler Stretch

2-4 Progressive, alternate sides

Primary Benefit: Stretches the hamstrings and low back.

Martial Arts Application: Improves kicking height and speed.

How to Perform:

1. Sit with your right leg bent to the side and your left leg extended in front of you.

2. Stretch forward to touch the toes of your left leg, keeping your toes pointed to the ceiling. Do not allow your foot to turn out.

Focus Point: Press your thigh into the floor and bend/rotate from the hip.

3. Turn and look to the back, rotating your upper body away from your left leg.

Caution: If you have knee pain or a pre-existing knee injury, try the beginner variation or discontinue the exercise. The traditional huddler stretch puts stress on the ligaments of the knee and can lead to instability of the knee joint.

Beginner variation:

1. Sit with your left leg folded in front of you and your right leg extended.

2. Stretch forward to touch the toes of your right leg, keeping your toes pointed toward the ceiling. Do not allow your toes to turn out.

3. If you cannot reach your toes, loop a belt around the arch of your foot and gently pull.

Partner variation:

1. Sit with your left leg folded in front of you and your right leg extended, keeping your toes pointed toward the ceiling.

2. Your partner places his hands on your lower back.

3. As you stretch forward toward your right foot, your partner pushes gently on your lower or mid-back to assist the stretch. Let your partner know when to stop pushing.

Hurdler Twist

2-4 Progressive, alternate sides

Primary Benefit: Stretches the muscles in the front and outside of the lower leg.

Martial Arts Application: Prepares the lower leg for deep stances and footwork.

How to Perform:

1. Sit with your left leg folded in front of you and your right outstretched.

2. Grasp your right foot with your right hand and rotate it slowly inward and toward you, so that your ankle faces upward. If you cannot reach your foot, use a towel to gently pull your foot inward and toward you.

Focus Point: Focus on keeping your buttocks flat on the floor.

Crossover Hurdler   *2-4 Progressive, alternate sides*

Primary Benefit: Stretches the back of the leg, particularly behind the knee, and in the lower back.

Martial Arts Application: Increases kicking range and height, especially raising kicks and kicks to the rear.

How to Perform:

1. Sit with your left leg outstretched and your right leg bent. Rest your left ankle above the knee of your right leg.

2. Bend forward at the waist and reach for your right foot.

Focus Point: Keep your toes pointed toward the ceiling and bend from your waist until you feel a gentle stretch behind your knee.

Side Split

2-4 Progressive, alternate sides

Primary Benefit: Stretches the legs and groin.

Martial Arts Application: Improves kicking height and range, especially for axe kick, crescent kicks, front kick, side kick and back kick.

How to Perform:

1. Extend your left leg in front of you and your right leg behind your body, keeping your knees straight.

2. For an added stretch, bend your upper body to the floor.

Focus Point: Focus on inhaling and exhaling deeply to release tension during the stretch. Create a feeling of dropping your upper body rather than pressing it downward.

Beginner variation:

If you cannot reach the floor, bend your rear leg and put your rear knee on the floor for support.

Easier

Seated Leg Extension

2-4 Progressive, alternate sides

Primary Benefit: Improves flexibility in the buttocks and hamstrings.

Martial Arts Application: Increases kicking height.

How to Perform:

1. Seated, grasp the arch of your right foot with you right hand and place your left hand on your right knee.

Focus Point: Gently round your spine to aid in releasing tension from your hamstrings.

2. Extend your leg by pulling with your right hand and pressing with your left. Press on your knee further to increase the stretch.

Center Split

2-4 Progressive

Primary Benefit: Stretches the legs and hip, particularly in the groin area.

Martial Arts Application: Improves kicking height and range.

How to Perform:

1. Sit with your legs split to either side, as far apart as is comfortable. Your knees should be straight but not locked out and your toes pointed toward the ceiling.

2. To deepen the stretch, move your hip and buttocks forward while keeping your feet in place.

Focus point: Focus on moving your hip forward while keeping your upper body erect and your toes pointed at the ceiling.

Beginner variation:

1. Begin with your feet flat on the floor, legs straight and your palms on the floor in front of you for support.

2. Slowly lower yourself down, shifting your weight onto your heels and pointing your toes toward the ceiling. Try to keep your back as erect as possible, using your arms to support yourself as necessary.

Deep Bow

2-4 Progressive, alternate sides

Primary Benefit: Stretches the muscles in buttocks and thighs.

Martial Arts Application: Improves flexibility for kicking (especially high side kick) and grappling.

How to Perform:

1. Sit with your right knee bent in front of you on the floor and your left knee folded gently behind you with your toes pointed.

Focus Point: Align your hip and knee along the same plane.

2. Lower your upper body forward over your right knee, resting your arms on the floor.

3. Keeping your right leg bent under you, stretch your left leg out straight behind with your toes pointed.

Caution: Do not perform this exercise if you have a preexisting knee injury or experience pain during the exercise.

Reach and Flex

8-10 Simple, alternate sides

Primary Benefit: Stretches the muscles of the hip and the quadriceps.

Martial Arts Application: Increases kicking height.

How to Perform:

1. Lie on your back with your arms outstretched and your knees bent.

2. Raise your right leg up toward the ceiling, pointing your toe and pulling your hip up off the floor. Balance your weight equally on your shoulders and left foot.

Focus Point: Focus on keeping your support knee at a ninety degree angle and your shoulders flat on the floor.

3. Pull your toes downward, flexing your foot and stretching the back of your leg. If you find it comfortable, you can also raise up onto the toes of your left foot.

Caution: Do not perform this exercise if you have a preexisting neck injury.

V Stretch

2-4 Progressive

Primary Benefit: Stretches the groin and leg muscles.

Martial Arts Application: Good preparation for kicking practice and a good way to work up to doing the more advanced splits.

How to Perform:

1. Lie on your back with your lower back flat to the floor and your legs raised up toward the ceiling, feet together.

2. Lower your legs to the sides. You may use your hands to gently support your legs or place your palms on the floor for balance.

Focus Point: Relax your feet so that your toes are lower than your heels.

Beginner variation:

1. If you find it difficult to keep your legs upright while stretching, lie down with your buttocks and legs resting against a wall.

2. Lower your legs along the wall, using the wall to support your feet, calves and thighs.

Prone Leg Extension

2-4 Progressive, alternate sides

Primary Benefit: Improves flexibility in the buttocks and hamstrings.

Martial Arts Application: Increases kicking height and range, especially for crescent kicks, front kick and axe kick.

How to Perform:

Lying on your back, grasp the arch of your left foot with your left hand and pull toward your left shoulder.

Focus point: Focus on keeping your hip equally balanced.

Caution: Place your hand or a belt in the arch of your foot. Do not pull on your toes during this exercise.

Easier

Beginner variation:

If you cannot grasp your foot, loop a belt around the arch of your foot and use it to gently pull your leg toward you.

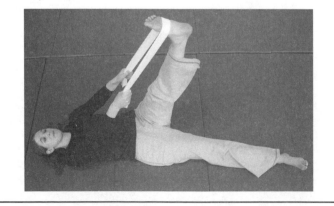

Double Leg Extension

6-8 Simple, alternate sides

Primary Benefit: Improves flexibility in the obliques, lower back, hip and buttocks.

Martial Arts Application: Improves flexibility for grappling, throwing and kicking.

How to Perform:

1. Lying on your back, extend your arms to the sides and raise both legs, keeping your knees straight.

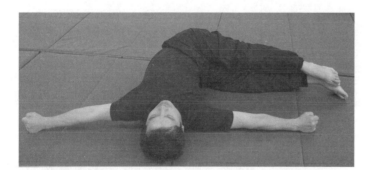

2. Slowly lower your legs to one side, as close to your outstretched hand as possible.

Focus Point: Use your arms to control the slow descent of your legs into the stretch.

Spinal Twist

2-4 Progressive, alternate sides

Primary Benefit: Stretches the lower back and buttocks.

Martial Arts Application: Improves flexibility for ground work and grappling.

How to Perform:

1. Lie on your back with your arms outstretched at shoulder height and your knees bent.

2. Cross your left leg over your right, placing your left ankle just above your right knee.

3. Lower your right knee to the floor on your right side and look to the left.

Focus point: Focus on keeping your shoulders and upper back flat on the floor.

Reverse Spinal Twist

2-4 Progressive, alternate sides

Primary Benefit: Stretches the lower back, buttocks and outer hip muscles.

Martial Arts Application: Improves flexibility for ground work and grappling.

How to Perform:

1. Lie on your back with your arms straight out to the side and your legs bent.

2. Cross your left leg over your right leg at the knee.

Focus point: Focus on keeping your shoulders and upper back flat on the floor for a maximum stretch in your hip and lower back muscles.

3. Use your left leg to gently pull your right leg toward the floor on the left side, while keeping your upper back and shoulders flat on the floor. Your lower back may twist slightly off the floor.

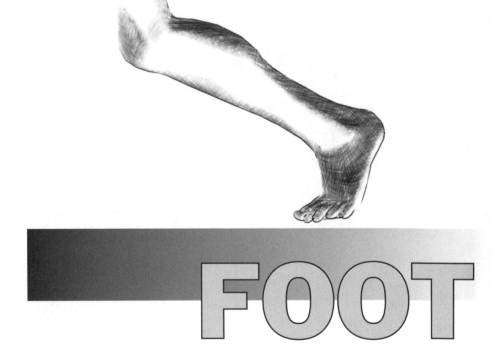

FOOT

Alternating Calf Stretch

8-12 Simple

Primary Benefit: Increases flexibility in the back of the lower leg.

Martial Arts Application: Improves jumping, pivoting, squatting, low stances and footwork.

How to Perform:

1. Bend forward (at about a 45° angle), staying on your toes, and place your palms on the ground.

2. Alternate touching your heels to the ground one at a time. If you cannot touch the ground, come as close as possible.

Focus Point: Pull your knees straight toward your head.

Heel Stretch

8-12 Simple

Primary Benefit: Increases flexibility in the back of the lower leg.

Martial Arts Application: Improves jumping, pivoting, squatting, low stances and footwork.

How to Perform:

1. Stand on a step and hold the railing or wall for balance.

2. With your heels hanging over the edge of the step, keep your legs straight and lower your heels.

Focus Point: Use your two feet as a unit, keeping your ankles and knees close together.

Caution: Do not perform this exercise if you have experienced plantar fasciitis in the past or if this exercise causes pain in your foot.

Instep Stretch

2-4 Progressive, alternate sides

Primary Benefit: Stretches the top of the foot up through the shin.

Martial Arts Application: Improves flexibility for kicks that use the top of the foot as a striking surface.

How to Perform:

1. Stand about arms' length from a wall and place your palms on the wall at shoulder height.

2. Reach back with one foot and place your toes on the floor.

3. Slowly sink into the stretch, pressing the top of your foot and ankle toward the floor.

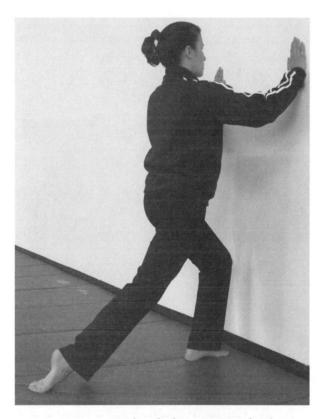

Focus Point: Slowly lower your body to increase the intensity of the stretch.

Arch Stretch

2-4 Progressive

Primary Benefit: Stretches the plantar arch on the bottom of the foot as well as the toes.

Martial Arts Application: Prepares the feet for kicking and footwork.

How to Perform:

1. Kneel on all fours, with your toes on the ground.

2. Slowly sit back toward your feet, keeping your toes pressed into the ground.

Focus Point: Keep your feet perpendicular to the floor. Do not allow your heels to turn outward.

Ankle Rotation

8-12 Simple, alternate sides

Primary Benefit: Loosens the ankle joint.

Martial Arts Application: Good warm-up for jumping, footwork and ground work.

How to Perform:

1. Sit with your left leg outstretched and your right leg resting on it.

2. Grasp your right foot with your left hand and gently rotate it to the left and then to the right.

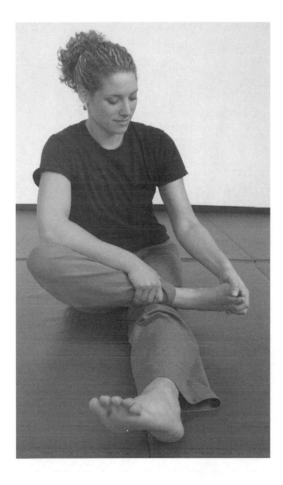

Focus Point: Begin with small natural circles and progress to wider rotations.

Toe Stretch

8-10 Simple

Primary Benefit: Loosens the muscles. of the feet.

Martial Arts Application: Good warm-up for jumping, footwork, kicking and ground work.

How to Perform:

1. Sit with your legs outstretched and your hands behind you for support.

2. Press your toes away from you and down toward the floor, keeping your ankles at a relaxed ninety-degree angle.

3. Pull your toes back toward your knees, keeping your ankles at a relaxed ninety-degree angle.

4. Relax your feet and spread your toes apart.

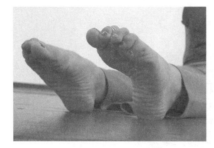 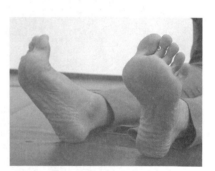

Focus Point: Give your full attention to your toes during this exercise. They are both the initiation and contact point of all kicks and are the precision element in footwork, kicking and stances.

Chapter
Seven

the Workouts

Core Workout

The Core Workout is where it all begins. Use these 15 stretches as your building blocks, adding style specific exercises as needed.

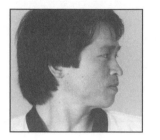

Neck Rotation (p. 105)

Shoulder Stretch (p. 113)

Finger Press (p. 151)

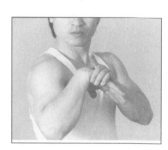

Wrist Flex (p. 149)

Standing Quad Stretch (p. 210)

Calf Stretch (p. 203)

Arch Stretch (p. 264)

Core Workout

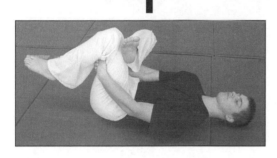

Elongation Stretch (p. 162)

Cross Knee Pull (p. 195)

Ankle Rotation (p. 265)

Lateral Chest Opening (p. 140)

Butterfly (p. 188)

Seated Torso Twist (p. 160)

Seated Toe Touch (p. 238)

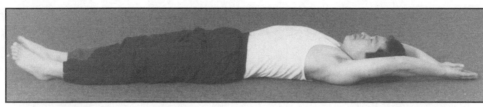

Warm Up

The goal of the warm up is to prepare the body for vigorous movement. Doing 8 - 12 repetitions of each exercise in this set will get your heart rate elevated and increase your body temperature in preparation for a workout. Begin with five minutes of aerobic exercises like footwork or light jogging.

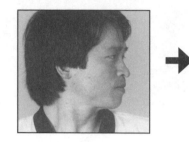

Neck Rotation (p. 105)

Arm Circles (p. 111)

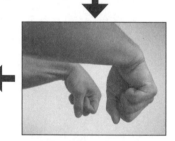

Finger Press (p. 151)

Side Bends (p. 155)

Half Windmills (p. 112)

Fist Roll (p. 153)

Moving Torso Bend (p. 157)

Arm Raises (p. 117)

Knee Rotation (p. 199)

Warm Up

Hip Rotation (p. 181)

Knee Raises (p. 200)

Leg Swings (p. 226)

Back Roll (p. 176)

Rear Leg Swings (p. 228)

Ankle Rotation (p. 265)

Alternating Calf Stretch (p. 261)

Cool Down

A brief cool down period allows your body to naturally return to its resting state. Perform each of the exercises in this set slowly, concentrating on your breathing and relaxing fully into each stretch.

Back Stretch (p. 174)

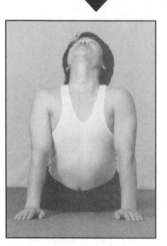

Chest Opening (p. 137)

Frog Stretch (p. 193)

Advanced Butterfly (p. 189)

Toe Stretch (p. 266)

Ankle Rotation (p. 265)

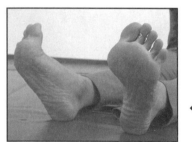

Back Curl (p. 177)

Shoulder Standing (p. 108)

Cool Down

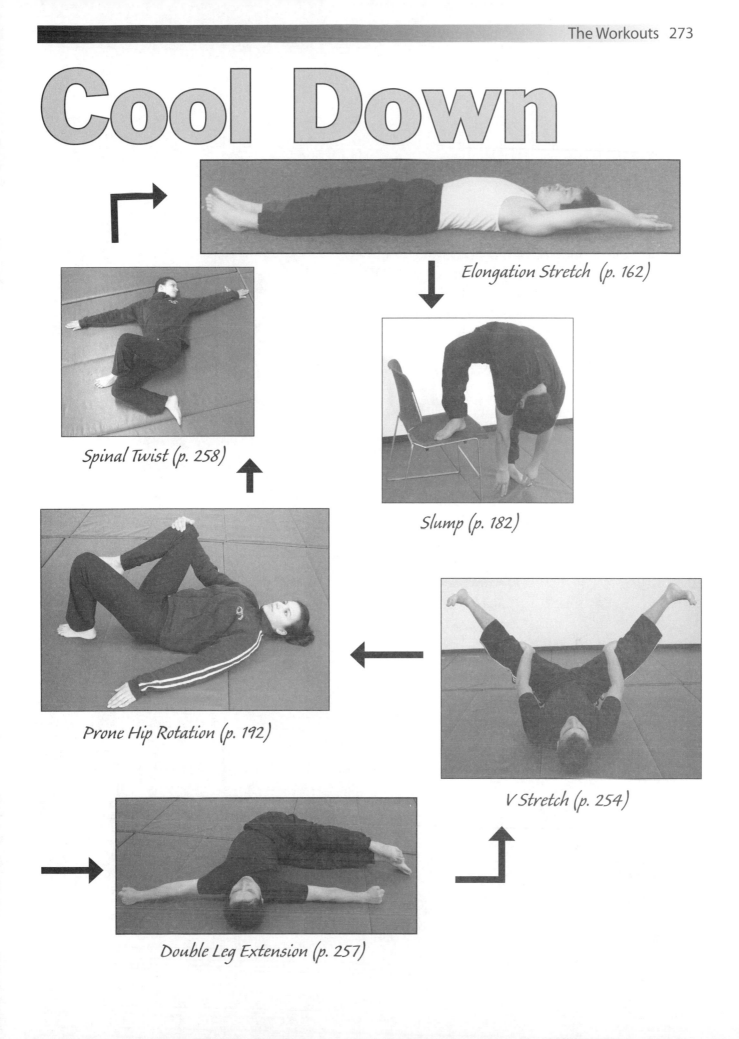

Elongation Stretch (p. 162)

Spinal Twist (p. 258)

Slump (p. 182)

Prone Hip Rotation (p. 192)

V Stretch (p. 254)

Double Leg Extension (p. 257)

Light Contact

If you practice a light or non-contact martial art like karate, kung fu, tai chi, kenpo, taekwondo or cardio kickboxing, supplement the core workout with stretches from this workout. Perform the core workout followed by the supplementary stretches or create your own workout by combining the two in a sequence that is comfortable for you.

Rear Arm Stretch (p. 116)

Twisting Toe Touch (p. 206)

Leg Swings (p. 226)

Seated Stick Twist (p. 173)

Leg Extension (p. 213)

Heel Stretch (p. 262)

Lunging Side Stretch (p. 166)

Knee Raises (p. 200)

Instep Stretch (p. 263)

Workout

Side Bends (p. 155)   *Chest Pull (p. 135)*   *Lying Torso Twist (p. 164)*

Partner Leg Raises (p. 216-221)

Back Curl (p. 177)   *Knee Pull (p. 190)*   *Kneeling Quad Stretch (p. 233)*

Groin Stretch (p. 230)   *V Stretch (p. 254)*

Full Contact

If you practice a full contact martial art like muay thai, karate, taekwondo or kickboxing, supplement the core workout with stretches from this workout. Perform the core workout followed by the supplementary stretches or create your own workout by combining the two in a sequence that is comfortable for you.

Rotator Cuff (p. 118)

Knee Raises (p. 200)

Groin Stretch (p. 230)

Single Arm Twist (p. 145)

Inside Forearm Stretch (p. 143)

Neck Pull (p. 106)

Instep Stretch (p. 263)

Chest Opening (p. 137)

Leg Swings (p. 226)

Workout

Measured Kicks (p. 229)

Modified Bridge (p. 107)

Controlled Kicks (p. 222-224)

Seated Stick Twist (p. 173)

Heel Stretch (p. 262)

Crossover Hurdler (p. 247)

Frog Stretch (p. 193)

V Stretch (p. 254)

Grappling

If you practice a grappling art like judo, hapkido, jujitsu or aikido, supplement the core workout with stretches from this workout. Perform the core workout followed by the supplementary stretches or create your own workout by combining the two in a sequence that is comfortable for you.

Outside Forearm Stretch (p. 144)

Neck Pull (p. 106)

Wrist Bend (p. 150)

Rotator Cuff (p. 118)

Kneeling Quad Stretch (p. 233)

Double Arm Pull (p. 114)

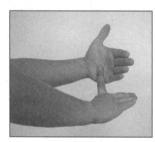

Finger Pull (p. 152)

Knee Pull (p. 190)

Single Arm Twist (p. 145)

Rear Palm Press (p. 119)

Workout

Rear Arm Stretch (p. 116)

Back Lift (p. 141)

Hurdler Twist (p. 246)

Bridge and Roll (p. 197)

Corner Press (p. 115)

Spinal Twist (p. 258)

Reverse Spinal Twist (p. 259)

Bridge (p. 168)

Modified Bridge (p. 107)

Mixed Martial

If you train for mixed martial arts competition in both stand-up and grappling skills, supplement the core workout with stretches from this workout. Perform the core workout followed by the supplementary stretches or create your own workout by combining the two in a sequence that is comfortable for you.

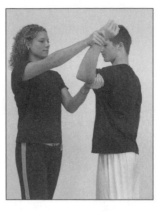

Rotator Cuff (p. 118)

Slump (p. 182)

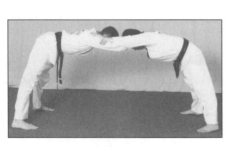

Partner Bridge (p. 128)

Single Arm Twist (p. 145)

Neck Pull (p. 106)

Back Lift (p. 141)

Knee Raises (p. 200)

Bridge (p. 168)

Instep Stretch (p. 263)

Full Body Arch (p. 163)

Art Workout

Knee Pull (p. 190)

Modified Bridge (p. 107)

Crossover Hurdler (p. 247)

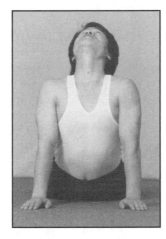

Chest Opening (p. 137)

Frog Stretch (p. 193)

Spinal Twist (p. 258)

Chest Pull (p. 135)

Squat (p. 187)

Leg Swings (p. 226)

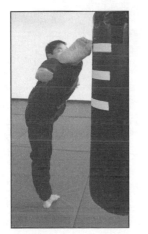

Measured Kicks (p. 229)

Back Stretch (p. 174)

Boxing

If you are a boxer or practice a punching based art, supplement the core workout with stretches from this workout. Perform the core workout followed by the supplementary stretches or create your own workout by combining the two in a sequence that is comfortable for you.

Neck Pull (p. 106)

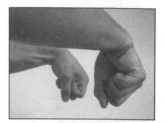

Fist Roll (p. 153)

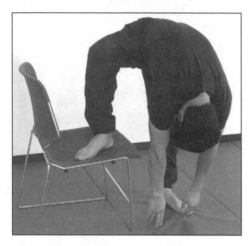

Slump (p. 182)

Single Arm Twist (p. 145)

Inside Forearm Stretch (p. 143)

Heel Stretch (p. 262)

Rotator Cuff (p. 118)

Corner Press (p. 115)

Squat (p. 187)

Torso Twist (p. 171)

Workout

Half Windmills (p. 112)

Spinal Twist (p. 258)

Arm Raises (p. 117)

Seated Stick
Twist (p. 173)

Chest Pull (p. 135)

Modified Bridge (p. 107)

Kneeling Reach (p. 122)

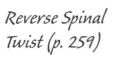

Reverse Spinal
Twist (p. 259)

Crossover Hurdler (p. 247)

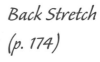

Back Stretch
(p. 174)

Weapons

If you practice a weapon such as the bo, nunchaku, joongbong or sword, supplement the core workout with stretches from this workout. Perform the core workout followed by the supplementary stretches or create your own workout by combining the two in a sequence that is comfortable for you.

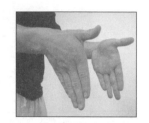

Wrist Bend (p. 150)

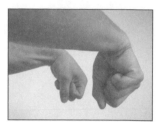

Fist Roll (p. 153)

Rear Towel Stretch (p. 120)

Partner Torso Twist (p. 159)

Torso Twist (p. 171)

Stick Lift (p. 125)

Kneeling Quad Stretch (p. 233)

Corner Press (p. 115)

Seated Stick Twist (p. 173)

Workout

Half Windmills (p. 112)

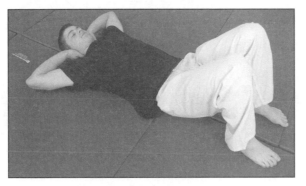

Shoulder Press (p. 136)

Stick Twist (p. 146)

Heel
Stretch
(p. 262)

Double Leg Extension (p. 257)

Rotator Cuff (p. 118)

Kneeling Reach (p. 122)

Kneeling
Forearm
Stretch (p. 123)

Back Stretch
(p. 174)

Single Arm Twist (p. 145)

High Kick

If increasing the height of your kicks is one of your goals, add a selection of exercises on this page to your regular stretching workout. Many of these exercises are advanced and assume that you are already at an intermediate to advanced level of flexibility. If you are a beginner, start with less intense variations.

Adv. Shoulder Standing (p. 109)

Kneeling Quad Stretch (p. 233)

Measured Kicks (p. 229)

Y Stretch (p. 194)

Advanced Butterfly (p. 189)

Side Bends (p. 155)

Adv. Lying Torso Twist (p. 165)

V Stretch (p. 254)

Knee Raises (p. 200)

Flexibility

Partner Leg Raises (p. 216–221)

Abductor Stretch (p. 202)

Lunging Side Stretch (p. 166)

Lateral Chest Opening (p. 144)

Leg Swings (p. 226)

Controlled Kicks (p. 222–224)

Alternating Calf Stretch (p. 261)

Straddle Stretch (p. 242)

Hurdler Twist (p. 246)

Standing Split (p. 231)

My Personal

1 I like doing this exercise before ground combat training because it helps me have confidence in my neck strength, especially for rear chokes or side headlocks. I do it for ten to thirty seconds for several sets. I usually combine this with the Bridge and Cat Stretch to enhance my back flexibility.

When I have stress or feel heavy, I do this for 3-5 minutes, then lower my feet to the floor above my head. It brings the blood from my lower legs to my head and loosens my lower body. Mentally, it makes me feel balanced. This exercise is also good for tumbling or ground combat practice. **2**

3 This exercise enhances oblique muscle flexibility. It makes me disoriented at the beginning but as I speed up I feel centered around the axle of my body. Coordination and spatial awareness can be surprisingly improved. I do it 20 to 100 times, especially before practicing spinning kicks.

4

Oblique muscles are the most important in circular kicks or punches, so I use this exercise to relax and stretch my side muscles before roundhouse or whip kicks. Usually I combine this with diagonal sit-ups to kill two birds: stretching and strengthening.

The wrist is very vulnerable in grappling. Either you lose or gain control of a fight by how you position your wrists. I combine this with the Wrist Flex, Finger Press and Fist Roll to gain sensitivity of wrist movements for offensive and defensive actions: pressing, breaking, circulating.

5

Top 10

6 I don't like to feel disoriented, so I disorient myself as much as I can before I engage in grappling or throwing. This is a safe, fun and challenging activity. I do it slowly and then fast 10 to 20 times. It is very important that you fix the vetical center of your body. I lower my center of gravity and spot his eyes before I touch hands.

This is a good exercise to release the tension in the hip joint and stretch your back and hamstring muscles. I especially like to do this after running. Position your feet in the most stable and comfortable position and just drop your body. Let gravity take over from there. **7**

8  Before practicing crescent kick, this is a must. I combine it with the Spinal Twist and Reverse Spinal Twist to release tension in the hip joint and low back that everyday activity alone can't resolve. The older you are, the more you might benefit from this sequence.

9

Nothing compares to actual kicking drills for kicking skills. Holding the bar provides me with feedback about my mistakes. When I do it slowly, I find it more difficult and I can be honest about my bad habits. Usually I combine this with leg swings at the bar.

10 A full split is what everyone wants to do. I find it is very important that I don't actually think about full stretch when I do it. I simply relax my mind, breathe deeply then gradually let my body succumb to the force of gravity.

Degree of Difficulty: Low

To assist you in choosing exercises for your training program, all of the exercises in the book have been ranked by difficulty level. The exercises listed on this page have a low degree of difficulty. They are well suited for those new to stretching, beginning martial artists and practitioners recovering from an injury or a prolonged period of time away from the arts.

Degree of Difficulty: Moderate

To assist you in choosing exercises for your training program, all of the exercises in the book have been ranked by difficulty level. The exercises listed on this page have a moderate degree of difficulty. They are well suited for intermediate students who want to increase their level of flexibility or advanced students who need a maintenance program.

Degree of Difficulty: High

To assist you in choosing exercises for your training program, all of the exercises in the book have been ranked by difficulty level. The exercises listed on this page have a high degree of difficulty. They are well suited for advanced students and elite athletes looking for a challenge. The exercises in this group should only be attempted when you feel confident in your ability to handle the associated risks. When in doubt, consult your instructor or begin with a less strenuous variation.

10 Tips: Full Split

While being able to do a split does not guarantee that you will be able to kick high, many martial artists like to perform splits as a measure of static flexibility. Here are 10 tips for achieving a full split:

1 In addition to practicing the split daily, create a stretching routine that targets the lower back, hip, groin and legs, specifically the following muscles: piriformis, psoas, adductor, abductor, hamstrings, quadriceps, gastrocnemius, soleus and Achilles tendon. See pages 64-70 for target exercises or choose from among the exercises on page 290 that target the split muscles.

2 If you experience pain in your hip or knees during a center split, tilt your pelvis forward. Tilting your pelvis will allow you to achieve a deeper split with less pressure on your joints.

3 Relax your upper body to promote relaxation in your lower body. Relaxation is the key to any stretch.

4 Sink your hips and legs into the ground by pressing downward once you have achieved your maximum stretch.

5 For a center split, there are two possible positions for your legs: knees facing the ceiling or knees turned forward. Depending on whether your hamstrings or groin muscles are more flexible, you might find one of these positions allows you to reach a full split sooner than the other.

6 You can ease the stretch in a front split by point your toes rather than pulling them back toward you. Pointing your toes will enable you to reach the floor more quickly.

7 During a front split, there are two possible positions for your rear leg: kneecap facing the floor or kneecap facing outward. Because they stretch different muscles, you may find that one position allows you to reach a full split sooner than the other. For either position, point the toes of the rear foot to avoid stressing the knee unnecessarily.

8 Begin from your most comfortable position. It is more important to achieve a moderate split with your legs straight, than to achieve a deeper split with your knees flexed. Condition your muscles to the correct posture early.

9 For a deeper stretch, gradually lean your body forward at the waist, supporting yourself with your hands, and then as you progress with your elbows. When you reach maximum flexibility, you will be able to touch your chest to the floor.

10 Breathe in through your nose, then exhale through your mouth as you lean forward or sink your hips and legs into the floor. Imagine emptying your body of air as you sink into the stretch.

20 Tips: High Kicks

1 Build strength with flexibility, both through kicking drills and resistance and flexibility training. One of the primary reasons high kicks are so challenging is the sheer weight of your leg. To propel the full weight of your leg into a vertical side kick relies as much on the strength of the muscles as on their range of motion.

2 Practice your high kicks as close to full speed as you are safely able to. Flexibility is speed-specific. Train your muscles to perform at the speed that you want them to perform.

3 Focus on dynamic flexibility training. Assuming you are an experienced martial artist, include the controlled, measured kick and leg swing exercises on pages 222-230 as a centerpiece of your high kick training.

4 If you are just beginning to train for high kicks, start out with the static exercises from the High Kick Workout on pages 286-287. Graduate to the dynamic excises in the High Kick Workout as well on pages 222-230 when you feel ready.

5 Use the inertia of your kicking leg to create power. Imagine using the large muscles of your thigh and buttocks to "throw" your foot at the target. Focus your kicking power in your thigh while keeping your foot relaxed until the moment of impact.

6 Bungee cord training (a bungee cord wrapped around your ankle and secured to the floor) builds flexibility in motion. Like running in sand or up hills, this type of training will build the large muscles of the leg in a very specific way. During bungee cord training, 75% of your regular kicking height is a good goal.

7 Use a doorframe to develop your kick structure. Place your foot and leg along the inside of one side of the doorframe and support your upper body on the other side. This will enable you to get a feel for correct alignment and posture in a static position. The doorframe provides both resistance and support for the upper and lower body.

8 Practice high kicking in motion. Rather than kicking from a static stance, imitate the rhythmic moving stances of Taekkyon or Capoeira practitioners. Find your body's natural rhythm and take advantage of it in achieving greater relaxation prior to high kicks.

9 Quick focused kicking movements are better suited to high kicks than large or slow movements. Chamber your leg quickly and compactly.

20 Tips: High Kicks

10 For high kick practice, you can achieve greater height by dropping your upper body to the rear during most high kicks, but in actually fighting situations, keep your upper body in a guarded posture.

11 Look at the target from start to finish.

12 Channel all of your power into raising your leg, then let your leg naturally return to it's chambered position. You don't need to put power into the retraction of the kick.

13 The knee of your standing leg should be slightly flexed, both to allow you to kick higher and to prevent knee injuries.

14 Imagine that your leg is like a hand holding a whip. The large muscles of your thigh and buttocks are the hand and the portion of your leg below the knee is the whip. Use the "hand" to whip your foot into the target.

15 Your standing foot should grab the floor. Stand firmly, but not flatfooted, actively rooting yourself to the floor.

16 Don't focus too much on any one part of the kick. Try to integrate all areas of your body and work toward a holistic movement.

17 Keep both arms bent and move them around the axis of your trunk. Opening your arms wide, letting them drop or overly tensing them draws energy away from your kick.

18 Your low stomach (danjun, dantien) is the center of your kick. When your leg goes up your head will go down. When your right side is up, your left is down. Focus on moving around this axis to maintain a constant center of gravity throughout the kick.

19 Practice on a hand target, sheet of paper, inner tube, speed bag or other light target.

20 The maximum force of a high kick is exerted just prior to impact. Whip the target rather than smashing through it. Kicking too hard will disrupt your balance and cause you to lose control of your kick after impact. Withdraw the kick immediately after impact, focusing on a light follow-through after the full dissipation of energy into the target.

Index

About the Author

Sang H. Kim is an internationally respected author of 9 martial arts books, including the best sellers *Ultimate Fitness through Martial Arts*, *Martial Arts After 40* and *1001 Ways to Motivate Yourself and Others*, and star of over 70 martial arts instructional videos/DVDs. He won the 1976 Korean National Champion and was named Instructor of the Year in Korea in 1983.

During his two decades of teaching martial arts in the US, he was featured in and his articles appeared in *Black Belt Magazine*, *The Journal of Asian Martial Arts*, *Delta Sky Magazine*, *Combat*, *Taekwondo Times* and over 100 other publications. He holds an M.S. degree in sports science and Ph.D. in media studies. He currently devotes his time to teaching, writing and presenting martial arts seminars for students and instructors in North America, Europe and Asia. He currently resides in Connecticut with his wife, daughter and beagle. He can be reached care of Turtle Press at www.turtlepress.com.

Also Available from Turtle Press:

Boxing: The American Martial Art
The Fighter's Body: An Owner's Manual
The Science of Takedowns, Throws and Grappling for Self-defense
Fighting Science
Martial Arts Instructor's Desk Reference
Guide to Martial Arts Injury Care and Prevention
Solo Training
Fighter's Fact Book
Conceptual Self-defense
Martial Arts After 40
Warrior Speed
The Martial Arts Training Diary for Kids
TeachingMartial Arts
Combat Strategy
The Art of Harmony
Total MindBody Training
1,001 Ways to Motivate Yourself and Others
Ultimate Fitness through Martial Arts
Weight Training for Martial Artists
A Part of the Ribbon: A Time Travel Adventure
Herding the Ox
Neng Da: Super Punches
Taekwondo Kyorugi: Olympic Style Sparring
Strike Like Lightning: Meditations on Nature

For more information:
Turtle Press
PO Box 290206
Wethersfield CT 06129-206
1-800-77-TURTL
e-mail: sales@turtlepress.com

http://www.turtlepress.com